THE
MODIFIED
KETO
COOKBOOK

Also by Dawn Marie Martenz
The Keto Cookbook

THE
MODIFIED
KETO
COOKBOOK

Quick, Convenient, Great-Tasting Recipes for Following a Low-Ratio Ketogenic Diet

Dawn Marie Martenz

with

Beth Zupec-Kania, RDN, CD

demosHEALTH

NEW YORK

Visit our website at www.demoshealth.com

ISBN: 978-1-936303-77-9
e-book ISBN: 978-1-61705-231-6

Acquisitions Editor: Julia Pastore
Compositor: DiacriTech

Medical information provided by Demos Health, in the absence of a visit with a health care professional, must be considered as an educational service only. This book is not designed to replace a physician's independent judgment about the appropriateness or risks of a procedure or therapy for a given patient. Our purpose is to provide you with information that will help you make your own health care decisions.

The information and opinions provided here are believed to be accurate and sound, based on the best judgment available to the authors, editors, and publisher, but readers who fail to consult appropriate health authorities assume the risk of injuries. The publisher is not responsible for errors or omissions. The editors and publisher welcome any reader to report to the publisher any discrepancies or inaccuracies noticed.

Library of Congress Cataloging-in-Publication Data
Martenz, Dawn Marie.
  The modified keto cookbook : quick, convenient great-tasting recipes for following a low-ratio ketogenic diet / Dawn Marie Martenz with Beth Zupec-Kania, RDN, CD.
    pages cm
  Includes bibliographical references and index.
  ISBN 978-1-936303-77-9
1. Ketogenic diet. I. Zupec-Kania, Beth. II. Title.
  RC374.K46M38 2015
  641.5'6383—dc23

                             2015028596

Special discounts on bulk quantities of Demos Health books are available to corporations, professional associations, pharmaceutical companies, health care organizations, and other qualifying groups. For details, please contact:

Special Sales Department
Demos Medical Publishing, LLC
11 West 42nd Street, 15th Floor
New York, NY 10036
Phone: 800-532-8663 or 212-683-0072
Fax: 212-941-7842
E-mail: specialsales@demosmedical.com

Printed in the United States of America by McNaughton & Gunn.

15 16 17 18 19 / 5 4 3 2 1

For Charlotte, my inspiration,
and everyone else who benefits from ketogenic diet therapies

CONTENTS

CHARLIE ABRAHAMS   1200CAL   3:1   PRO21 FAT 116.1 CHO 17.1

MEAL PLAN

Amounts of protein, fat, and carbohydrate
are in the same ratio at each meal and
therefore the meals may be used interchange-
ably.

PLAN 1

- 17 GMS BREAST OF CHICKEN
- 18 GMS COOKED MACARONI
- 28 GMS FAT
- 50 GMS 36% CREAM

PLAN 2

- 15 GMS CHICKEN BREAST
- 9 GMS HAVARTI CHEESE
- 29 GMS BOILED POTATO
- 47 GMS FAT

PLAN 3

- 22 GMS BUMBLE BEE SOLID WHITE TUNA
- 24 GMS MACARONI OR SPAHETTI (COOKED)
- 53 GMS FAT
- 1 LETTUCE LEAF

PLAN 4

- 51 GMS HEB. NATIONAL BEEF FRANK
- 21 GMS COOKED MACARONI
- 33 GMS FAT
- 1 LETTUCE LEAF

PLAN 5

- 28 GMS EGG
- 6 GMS CRISP BACON
- 20 GMS FAT
- 37 GMS 10% FRUIT
- 12 GMS SOUR CREAM
- 40 36% CREAM

WHIP CREAM
ADD FRUIT
SOUR CREAM
FREEZE TO MAKE
YOGURT

PLAN 6

- 40 GMS BOB EVANS SAUSAGE
- 15 GMS. BOILED POTATO
- 10 GMS FAT
- 50 GMS 36% CREAM
- 6 GMS BAKERS CHOC
(TO MAKE HOT CHOC)

FRUIT OR JUICE: FRESH OR CANNED WITHOUT SUGAR

10%

Applesauce, Motts	Papaya
Cantaloupe	Peach
Grapefruit	Strawberries
Grapes, purple	Tangerine
Honeydew melon	Watermelon
Orange	

15%: Use 2/3 the amount of 10% fruit prescribed.

Apple	Nectarine
Apricot	Pear
Blackberries	Pineapple
Blueberries	Plums, Damson
Figs	Rasberries, black
Grapes, green	Rasberries, red
Mango	Kewi

Drained fruits, frozen or canned without
sugar may be used. If the juice is used it
must be included in the weight. No dried
fruits should be used.

VEGETABLES: FRESH, CANNED OR FROZEN

Raw or cooked as specified

GROUP A: (use twice the amount prescribed)

Asparagus - C	Radish - R
Beet greens - C	Rhubarb - R
Cabbage - C	Sauerkraut - C
Celery - C or R	Summer squash - C
Chicory - R	Swiss chard - C
Cucumbers - R	Tomato - R
Eggplant - C	(or juice)
Endive - R	Turnips - C
Green pepper - R or C	Turnip greens - C
Poke - C	Watercress - R

GROUP B: (use amount prescribed)

Beets - C	Kohlrabi - C
Broccoli - C	Mushrooms - R
Brussel sprouts - C	Mustard greens - C
Cabbage - R	Okra - C
Carrots - R or C	Onions - R or C
Cauliflower - C	Rutabagas - C
Collards - C	Spinach - C
Dandelion greens - C	Tomato - C
Green beans - C	Winter squash - C
Kale - C	

FAT SUBSTITUTIONS:

Bacon fat	Mayonnaise
Butter	Oil*
Margarine*	

*Polyunsaturated fats (Safflower, Sunflower
or corn) are recommended. Allotted fat may
be mixed in with foods, i.e., mayonnaise
with egg, melted margarine over vegetables
and/or meat.

**All foods must be weighed after cooking
or as directed on menus.

Keto Cookbook, circa 1993

Foreword

To fully appreciate Dawn Marie Martenz's *The Modified Keto Cookbook*, please take a look at a page from our family's "keto cookbook," circa 1993. Back then, the very notion that delicious recipes could be designed, calculated, prepared, and beautifully photographed for us in advance would have been unimaginable. The fact that dishes would be organized into breakfast, lunch, dinner, side dishes, and dessert selections would have been such a relief and saved so much time. The ability to involve the whole family in meal preparation and dining together with meals that looked similar to what Charlie was eating would have made dinnertime far less stressful for the whole family. Charlie's brother and sister would not have had to hide and eat behind Charlie's back so that he would not see what they were eating and what he could not have. Even the notion that there was an entire community out there that was in need of this information would have chipped away at the isolation we felt with a child on the ketogenic diet.

Dawn's passion as Charlotte's keto mom for seven years, coupled with Beth Zupec-Kania RDN, CD's expertise working with diet therapy for over 20 years worldwide, have created an invaluable tool for any keto family.

There is no doubt that *The Modified Keto Cookbook* will remain an indispensable resource for as long as your keto days continue.

Nancy and Jim Abrahams

Charlie's parents,
Founders of The Charlie Foundation for Ketogenic Therapies

Introduction

In 2010, my family was introduced to the world of ketogenic diet therapies. Our five-year-old daughter, Charlotte, started a classic 4:1 ratio ketogenic diet to hopefully control the hundreds of seizures she was experiencing daily. Charlotte was diagnosed with Dravet's Syndrome when she was 21 months old, and we had tried nearly every possible antiepileptic medication available in the United States. We even tried medications purchased from Canada and France. Nothing worked. Even her rescue medications stopped working, resulting in numerous nonstop seizure episodes or "status seizures." Charlotte started the ketogenic diet while an in-patient at Children's National Medical Center in Washington, DC. She began the hospital stay having myoclonic seizures about every two to three seconds, increasing to full tonic–clonic seizures by the early evening. By the third day in the hospital her body had converted to ketosis and she was experiencing zero seizures. My husband and I held our breath, waiting for epilepsy to rear it's ugly head again, but it didn't. The diet was working.

Since that hospital stay, Charlotte has continued to grow and progress while on the ketogenic diet. Over the past five plus years she has gradually weaned from a 4:1 ratio to a liberal 2:1 ratio. She still experiences an occasional tonic–clonic seizure, mostly when she is ill, but the ketogenic diet has given her a chance to live her life to the fullest. In retrospect, Hippocrates' sentiments captured the essence of the ketogenic diet when he said, "let food be thy medicine and medicine be thy food." It has been amazing to experience Charlotte's success with the diet—with food as her best medicine.

Familiar and simple, was the mantra I had while selecting and creating the recipes for this book. Like many other people, we began the ketogenic diet in the midst of experiencing a health crisis. I know from experience how stressful it can be to put food on the table while your mind is preoccupied with so many other things. Over the years my family has found new favorite meals and moved toward a "whole foods" approach to eating. In my time working with The Charlie Foundation, a 501(c)(3) nonprofit that advocates for ketogenic diet therapies treating epilepsy, neurological disorders, and cancers, I have spoken with many people who are on or beginning ketogenic diet therapies. Almost everyone has two things in common: they need ketogenic food and it needs to taste good enough to eat. It also helps if it can be made quickly, easily, and in bulk. Some people are not great home cooks and have relied on convenience foods and eating out. Many people are strapped for time and find it hard to juggle making everything from scratch. Others just don't like to cook! Lots of people don't want to give up their favorite things to eat. Yes, the diet can be hard, and it takes time to adjust to a new style of cooking and eating. But when your life or that of a loved one depends on it, it is worth the effort.

How to Use This Book

First and most importantly, please respect that ketogenic diets are metabolic therapies which require medical supervision for safety. As with any metabolic diet therapy, there can be adverse effects if not managed with appropriate supplementation and monitoring. It is highly recommended that anyone who follows a ketogenic diet regularly consult with a qualified nutritionist. They will be able to monitor for possible side effects and help determine the appropriate amount of calories, protein, carbohydrate, and fat. For more detailed information about the basic guidelines for following a modified ketogenic diet, please read *Modified Ketogenic Diet Therapy, 1:1 and 2:1 Prescriptions* written by Beth Zupec-Kania RDN, CD, from The Charlie Foundation. This is an inexpensive booklet available in The Charlie Foundation store at www .charliefoundation.org.

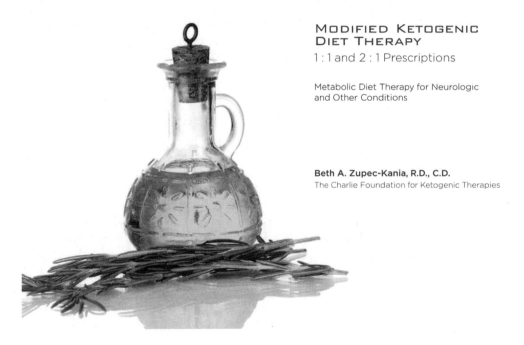

MODIFIED KETOGENIC
DIET THERAPY

1 : 1 and 2 : 1 Prescriptions

Metabolic Diet Therapy for Neurologic
and Other Conditions

Beth A. Zupec-Kania, R.D., C.D.
The Charlie Foundation for Ketogenic Therapies

All the recipes in this cookbook are calculated using the KetoDietCalculator©, a web-based database created by Beth Zupec-Kania, RDN, CD. The KetoDietCalculator is a ketogenic diet planning tool provided by The Charlie Foundation, without fee, to licensed nutritionists. Nutritionists who obtain access are able to provide detailed nutrition guidelines to their patients who are then able to calculate meals and snacks. Nutritional information in the KetoDietCalculator is derived from the USDA Database and food manufacturers. All meal plans in the KetoDietCalculator are calculated in gram weights. If you are currently using the KetoDietCalculator, please use the gram weights provided in the recipes as a guideline. Many manufactured food items differ slightly in nutrition and may not match exactly once calculated. The KetoDietCalculator can be found at www.ketodietcalculator.org.

What is a "ratio"? In the nutrition information for each recipe you will notice the "ratio" number is included. Some very high-fat recipes will have a number as high as 25:1, and very low-fat, higher-carb recipes will have a significantly lower number, such as 0.6:1. Very simply, this is the number of fat grams for every 1 gram of protein plus carbohydrate. For example, a 4:1 ratio means there are 4 grams of fat for every gram of protein and carbohydrate combined. The higher the first number is, the higher the fat content of the recipe is.

Many readers who use this book will not have access to the KetoDietCalculator. That is OK! Common U.S. household measurements such as cups and tablespoon amounts have been included as well. For 2:1 ratio diets and below, it is possible to use common measurements and still produce a reliable ketogenic recipe. It is important to follow the measurement guidelines given in the recipe regarding mincing, dicing, or slicing. One cup of cucumber that is diced will weigh less than one cup of cucumber that has been minced because there is less space between the cucumber pieces, therefore allowing more cucumber to fit into the measuring cup. Most of the estimated weights for food item measurements have been derived from the USDA Database. Others have been taken from manufacturers' packaging. Take your time to measure correctly to ensure the most accurate nutritional content.

Many of the recipes make large "family size" meals, especially the dinner recipes. The person who is following a ketogenic diet will be able to eat a portion from the main dish. For others who are not following a ketogenic diet, additional sides such as rice, pasta, or extra vegetables may be included. What's important is that the person who requires a ketogenic meal is able to eat and enjoy the same meal as everyone else. If you don't want to serve the recipes to the rest of the family, cook the entire batch and save the extra portions for later. Many of the recipes freeze wonderfully and taste just as good when reheated. This can be especially helpful for very busy individuals.

Most of the breakfast and lunch recipes are single serving portions. People tend to eat the same few meals for breakfast and lunch. When they find something they like they stick with it! Be sure to try to include as many vegetables as possible. Breakfast and lunch offer many possibilities for including vegetables. Spaghetti squash is almost always hidden in eggs, salad does not always mean just lettuce, and the Green Smoothie can be a nutrition boost to help include a daily dose of dark leafy greens.

Many of the sauces and desserts are rich and abundant sources of fat! How great is it to boost your daily fat intake with a serving of vanilla pudding or a bite of coconut filled chocolates? The sauce recipes have suggested serving sizes to give an idea of the calories and fat grams. If needed, add more fat to your meal. Use the recipes as guidelines and adjust them to fit your needs for nutrition and flavor.

One of the most important things to remember when following ketogenic diet therapy is to always read labels! The nutrition information presented in this book reflects labels and information from manufacturers as available at the time of printing.

Companies frequently change ingredients, and these changes will result in nutritional variations of the recipes. If a specific brand is noted in a recipe, please try to use it. If another brand is substituted, the nutritional information will also be altered.

I hope you enjoy the recipes in this book. It has been a wonderful experience to include our daughter in family meals again while still maintaining a style of eating that is best for her health. Whether you are just beginning your journey into ketogenic therapies, or you are recently enjoying a more liberal version of the diet, hopefully you will find recipes you enjoy. Ketogenic diets don't have to be complicated: eat vegetables, just enough protein, and add plenty of fat.

THE
MODIFIED
KETO
COOKBOOK

THE KETO PANTRY

While following a ketogenic diet, your pantry should look like a natural food store! Brightly colored boxes of cereal, packages of processed snacks and sweets, and pre-made heat-and-serve meals should disappear. The majority of ingredients in this cookbook are "whole foods," meaning they are fats, proteins, vegetables, and fruits in a mostly unprocessed or minimally processed state. The bulk of food while on a ketogenic diet should come from whole foods.

FRESH PRODUCE

Choose a wide variety of fruits and vegetables to eat on a daily basis. Try to include as many vegetables as possible, even adding them to breakfast. While shopping, choose the most vibrant colored produce that is not wilted or damaged. Use the produce scales in the grocery store to help determine how much to buy. Choose organic if you can, but do not let the extra cost prohibit you from buying what you need. It is better to eat conventional (nonorganic) produce than to eat a limited or smaller amount of organic produce.

Don't forget the frozen produce! Many minimally processed fruits and vegetables are available in the freezer section of grocery stores. Frozen vegetables offer peak nutritional values since they are picked fresh and then flash frozen. Always choose products that have no added ingredients.

LOW-CARBOHYDRATE FLOUR REPLACEMENTS

Almond meal, coconut flour, arrowroot starch, flaxseed meal, shredded coconut, oat bran, and xanthan gum are used for baked goods. It is usually a blend of several of these ingredients that produces the best result. Arrowroot, flaxseed meal, and xanthan gum help replace the gluten in baked goods and provide flexibility and sponginess. Although many of these ingredients may be more costly than traditional flours, you use significantly less and the product will last longer before running out.

SWEETENERS

Two different types of sweeteners are used in this book: powdered Truvia and liquid stevia. As a general rule of thumb, Truvia tastes better in baked items or recipes that are heated. Liquid stevia is best used in cold food and recipes. Heat seems to highlight the bitterness of liquid stevia. This, of course is a matter of personal preference. If you like liquid stevia, please use it and omit the Truvia. Truvia contains erythritol (a sugar alcohol) and therefore is higher in carbohydrates. Please adjust the sweetness in the recipes to suit your taste preferences. You may start a ketogenic diet by requiring more sweetener than what is recommended in the recipes, but over time you will need less as your taste adjusts to a low-carbohydrate (and sugar) diet.

HERBS AND SPICES

Having fresh and flavorful herbs and spices is the best way to add flavor and variety to your recipes. It is highly recommended that you clean out your spice cabinet and discard anything that has been in there for more than one year. Seasoning "packets" should never be used: they often contain fillers and thickeners such as cornstarch, which is high in carbohydrates; they often add sweeteners as well. Make sure that your herbs and spices contain 100% of the herb or spice and no fillers.

If you find that you are not using an entire jar of herbs or spices in one year, save your money and buy smaller quantities. Seek out a spice store near you or online; the quality and freshness of the spices are far superior to grocery store brands. If you do not have a spice store near you, order fresh herbs and spices from Penzeys at www.penzeys.com. Do not overlook the importance of salt while cooking. The recipes in this book have all been tested using kosher salt unless otherwise noted.

FATS

In the following recipes, you will see lots of extra virgin olive oil, butter, and coconut oil. Try to use the best quality fats you can afford. Since the majority of calories come from fat when following a ketogenic diet, it is important to use good quality fats from a wide variety of sources that offer different nutritional properties. Try to use fats in the most unrefined, natural state as possible. The more refined an oil or fat is, the less nutrition it has to offer. Plant-based fats such as avocados and olives, flaxseeds and hempseeds, and nuts such as macadamia and pecans are fantastic to include in ketogenic diets—they offer an "all in one" combination that includes fat, protein, and fiber. Don't be afraid to branch out of your comfort zone and try a type of oil or fat that you have not used before.

BREAKFAST

Fiber Rolls 2.0

Yogurt Base

Awesome Waffles

Breakfast Porridge

Cinnamon Granola

Basic Quiche

Breakfast Taco

Breakfast Casserole

Chocolate Peanut Butter Breakfast Shake

Green Smoothie

Baked Eggs with Cream and Herbs

Blueberry Almond Spoonbread

Fiber Rolls 2.0

NUTRITION FACTS   **Makes 4 Servings**

Serving Size: ¼ of the recipe

Each Serving Provides:

2:1 Ratio

Calories: 161

Carbohydrate: 1.77 grams

Protein: 5.52 grams

Fat: 14.63 grams

Fiber Rolls are a low-carb bread recipe dream come true! They are light in texture, fluffy, moist, pliable, and tasty. You do not have to miss out on a serving of bread to go along with a meal. Shape the dough from this recipe into any size or shape you would like. You can make an Italian style loaf for slicing, individual mini dinner rolls, flat sandwich or hamburger rounds, or even a pizza crust or thin roll-up. Do not be intimidated; try this recipe! It is as simple as mixing wet ingredients with dry. You can even use an electric hand mixer.

Do not eliminate or adjust any ingredient, no matter how insignificant it may seem. This recipe has been tested many times and minor adjustments make a big impact. With that said, it is best to weigh the ingredients on a gram scale. Even though standard measurements are provided, they are not nearly as accurate as weight.

Please note that this recipe contains psyllium husks. Psyllium is a "bulking" fiber that absorbs large quantities of liquid, quickly expanding in size. Please drink plenty of water when consuming psyllium and follow dietary guidelines for amounts of psyllium to consume depending on your age.

Dry ingredients:

21 grams or 3 tablespoons flaxseed meal

12 grams or 4 teaspoons psyllium powder

10 grams or 2 teaspoons coconut flour

7 grams or 1½ teaspoons Truvia (2 packets)

1 gram or ¼ teaspoon baking soda

1 gram or ¼ teaspoon baking powder

⅛ teaspoon xanthan gum

⅛ teaspoon salt

Wet ingredients:

100 grams or 2 large eggs

56 grams or ¼ cup (2 ounces) full-fat cream cheese, room temperature

20 grams or 1 tablespoon plus 1 teaspoon melted coconut oil

10 grams or 2 teaspoons cider vinegar

10 grams or 2 teaspoons warm water

1. Preheat the oven to 350°F. Line a baking sheet with parchment paper.

2. In a small bowl, combine all of the dry ingredients. Break up any lumps of coconut flour.

3. Combine all of the wet ingredients in a mixing bowl large enough to use an electric hand mixer. Beat all the ingredients together until most of the lumps of cream cheese are gone. Scrape the sides once and beat again to combine.

4. Add the dry ingredients to the wet. Start the mixer on very slow speed to combine. Beat the dough on full speed until it is smooth. You will notice it thickening very quickly. Scrape the sides once. Do not mix for longer than 30 seconds.

5. Quickly scrape the dough out of the mixing bowl onto the lined baking sheet. Using wet hands to prevent sticking, divide the dough and shape as desired. The dough will rise about double its original size.

6. Bake the dough. If shaped into one loaf, 2 inches wide by 8 inches long, baking will take about 35 to 40 minutes. Smaller rolls and thin sandwich rounds will take about 20 to 30 minutes. The bread is done when the inside is dry and the center is firm—when a toothpick is inserted, it should come out clean. The rolls should not deflate or collapse after baking. If this happens, the bread was not cooked long enough.

▶ To make crackers or croutons, cut the dough into thin slices and place on a lined baking sheet. You may season with dried herbs and spices if desired. Bake at 300°F for 30 to 45 minutes or until crisp. Flip the slices at least once during baking to help them cook evenly. When they are almost crisp enough, turn the oven off and let them cool inside the oven with the door closed. Store in an airtight bag or plastic container for up to one week.

Yogurt Base

NUTRITION FACTS   **Makes 9 Servings**

Recipe Yields: 3 cups

Serving Size: ⅓ cup

Each Serving Provides:

1.9:1 Ratio

Calories: 197

Carbohydrate: 3.01 grams

Protein: 6.34 grams

Fat: 17.75 grams

This combination of ingredients produces a perfectly smooth and thick yogurt base without altering the tart flavor of plain yogurt. The yogurt mixture may be eaten plain or with a few drops of liquid stevia, fresh or frozen berries, or the fruit concentrates found on pages 7 to 10 for flavor and sweetness.

500 grams or 1 (17.6 ounce) container Fage Total 2% yogurt

212 grams or 1 (7.5 ounce) container of crème fraiche (full-fat)

72 grams or ⅓ cup extra light tasting olive oil

Optional: 3 liquid stevia drops per serving

1. Combine all ingredients in a mixing bowl. Add liquid stevia drops if using. Stir very well to combine.
2. Divide mixture into nine individual containers, cover, and store in the refrigerator. Add additional fruit toppings just prior to serving.

Fruit Concentrates

On their own these fruit concentrates will be too overpowering, but when added to the yogurt base (page 6) they provide the perfect balance of tart and sweet. For citrus concentrates, use fresh squeezed citrus juice only!

The method is the same for each flavor. The nutrition information will vary slightly for each.

Lemon Concentrate

NUTRITION FACTS (served with ⅓ cup yogurt base) Makes 8 Servings

Recipe Yields: ½ cup concentrate

Serving Size: 1 tablespoon

Each Serving Provides:

2.14:1 Ratio

Calories: 230

Carbohydrate: 3.53 grams

Protein: 6.36 grams

Fat: 21.12 grams

NUTRITION FACTS (no yogurt, concentrate only) Makes 8 Servings

Recipe Yields: ½ cup concentrate

Serving Size: 1 tablespoon

Each Serving Provides:

6.18:1 Ratio

Calories: 33

Carbohydrate: 0.52 grams

Protein: 0.03 grams

Fat: 3.39 grams

61 grams or ¼ cup freshly squeezed lemon juice

27 grams or ⅛ cup extra light tasting olive oil

3.5 grams or ¾ teaspoon Truvia (1 packet)

0.5 grams or ⅛ teaspoon xanthan gum

⅛ cup water

1. Combine all ingredients in a small glass bowl. Stir very well to combine. The xanthan gum will continue to thicken the mixture as it sits. Add 1 tablespoon to yogurt just prior to eating.

2. Store the concentrate in a covered glass jar in the refrigerator for up to one week.

Lime Concentrate

NUTRITION FACTS (served with ⅓ cup yogurt base) Makes 8 Servings

Recipe Yields: ½ cup concentrate

Serving Size: 1 tablespoon

Each Serving Provides:

2.11:1 Ratio

Calories: 230

Carbohydrate: 3.63 grams

Protein: 6.37 grams

Fat: 21.11 grams

NUTRITION FACTS (no yogurt, concentrate only) Makes 8 Servings

Recipe Yields: ½ cup concentrate

Serving Size: 1 tablespoon

Each Serving Provides:

5.1:1 Ratio

Calories: 33

Carbohydrate: 0.63 grams

Protein: 0.03 grams

Fat: 3.38 grams

61 grams or ¼ cup freshly squeezed lime juice

27 grams or ⅛ cup extra light tasting olive oil or grape-seed oil. Grape-seed oil has a natural green color that will enhance the green color of the lime concentrate.

3.5 grams or ¾ teaspoon Truvia (1 packet)

0.5 grams or ⅛ teaspoon xanthan gum

⅛ cup water

1. Combine all ingredients in a small glass bowl. Stir very well to combine. The xanthan gum will continue to thicken the mixture as it sits. Add 1 tablespoon to yogurt just prior to eating.

2. Store the concentrate in a covered glass jar in the refrigerator for up to one week.

Orange Concentrate

NUTRITION FACTS (served with ⅓ cup yogurt base) Makes 8 Servings

Recipe Yields: ½ cup concentrate

Serving Size: 1 tablespoon

Each Serving Provides:

2.01:1 Ratio

Calories: 232

Carbohydrate: 4.10 grams

Protein: 6.41 grams

Fat: 21.12 grams

NUTRITION FACTS (no yogurt, concentrate only) Makes 8 Servings

Recipe Yields: ½ cup concentrate

Serving Size: 1 tablespoon

Each Serving Provides:

2.9:1 Ratio

Calories: 35

Carbohydrate: 1.10 grams

Protein: 0.07 grams

Fat: 3.40 grams

83 grams or ⅓ cup freshly squeezed orange juice

27 grams or ⅛ cup extra light tasting olive oil

3.5 grams or ¾ teaspoon Truvia (1 packet)

0.5 grams or ⅛ teaspoon xanthan gum

1. Combine all ingredients in a small glass bowl. Stir very well to combine. The xanthan gum will continue to thicken the mixture as it sits. Add 1 tablespoon to yogurt just prior to eating.
2. Store the concentrate in a covered glass jar in the refrigerator for up to one week.

Coconut Concentrate

NUTRITION FACTS (served with ⅓ cup yogurt base) Makes 8 Servings

Recipe Yields: ½ cup concentrate

Serving Size: 1 tablespoon

Each Serving Provides:

2:1 Ratio

Calories: 213

Carbohydrate: 3.19 grams

Protein: 6.51 grams

Fat: 19.34 grams

NUTRITION FACTS (no yogurt, concentrate only) Makes 8 Servings

Recipe Yields: ½ cup concentrate

Serving Size: 1 tablespoon

Each Serving Provides:

4.53:1 Ratio

Calories: 16

Carbohydrate: 0.18 grams

Protein: 0.17 grams

Fat: 1.61 grams

¼ cup water plus up to an additional ¼ cup water

20 grams or 4 tablespoons dried, shredded coconut, unsweetened

0.2 grams or 1 pinch xanthan gum

5 liquid stevia drops or enough to suit your taste

2 to 3 drops coconut extract (optional, but will enhance the coconut flavor significantly)

1. In a 1 cup glass measuring cup, combine all of the ingredients except the additional water. Stir very well to combine, making sure there are no lumps.

2. Cover the bowl with plastic wrap and let the coconut sit for two hours or longer to hydrate.

3. After two hours, stir the coconut mixture and add enough of the additional water to reach ½ cup. Continue to stir. Taste the coconut mixture for sweetness; add a few more drops of stevia if needed. Add 1 tablespoon of coconut concentrate to yogurt just prior to eating.

4. Store the concentrate in a covered glass jar in the refrigerator for up to one week.

Awesome Waffles

NUTRITION FACTS **Makes 2 Servings**

Serving Size: ½ of a 9-inch waffle (half of the batch)

Each Serving Provides:

1.59:1 Ratio

Calories: 208

Carbohydrate: 4.83 grams

Protein: 6.52 grams

Fat: 18.03 grams

Waffles are truly one of the hardest recipes to replicate for low-carb and ketogenic diets. Arrowroot flour is what makes this recipe light, fluffy, and chewy. The sour cream and vinegar help replace the buttermilk "tang." Don't skip the vinegar; it is critical to the final flavor. Enjoy these on a slow weekend morning, spread with butter and a side of protein. If you absolutely need a form of syrup, Walden Farms makes a very low-carb syrup substitute, but it is highly processed so it would be considered an "occasional" ingredient.

The recipe will be most reliable when ingredients are weighed on a gram scale. Waffle irons vary widely, but you will want to set it on the lowest setting possible. Ignore any alarms or whistles and pay attention to the steam. The waffles will take longer to cook than regular ones and they will be ready when most of the steam has stopped coming out of the waffle maker.

Sift your almond flour before weighing. For the best results, use the most finely ground almond flour. Some almond flour can have larger pieces that will remain gritty and crunchy in the batter.

14 grams or 1 tablespoon butter, melted

50 grams or 1 large egg

30 grams or 2 tablespoons full-fat sour cream

5 grams or 1 teaspoon cider vinegar

28 grams or ¼ cup almond flour

6 grams or 2 teaspoons arrowroot flour

3.5 grams or ¾ teaspoon Truvia (1 packet)

0.5 grams or ⅛ teaspoon baking powder

0.5 grams or ⅛ teaspoon baking soda

0.1 grams or a pinch xanthan gum

Pinch of salt

1. Melt the butter in a small bowl. Add the egg, sour cream, and vinegar to the butter. Stir to combine.

2. Sift the dry ingredients into the wet. Stir very well until all lumps have dissolved.

3. Pour the batter into a preheated waffle iron and bake on the lowest setting until there is very little steam coming out of the waffle iron. When the waffle iron has stopped steaming, carefully remove the waffle by piercing the side with a fork and lifting it out.

4. Most likely the bottom half of the waffle will be the "prettier" side. Serve half of the waffle spread with butter for additional fat, if needed, and a side of protein.

Breakfast Porridge

NUTRITION FACTS   **Makes 2 Servings**

Recipe Yields: 1 cup	Calories: 222
Serving Size: ½ cup	Carbohydrate: 3.90 grams
Each Serving Provides:	Protein: 2.68 grams
3.31:1 Ratio	Fat: 21.78 grams

A warm, comforting hot cereal for a cold morning. Blend the coconut in a blender for a finer texture. If the porridge is made in advance, the coconut will be even softer. Add additional protein to make a complete meal; eggs (cooked any way) and bacon are delicious!

20 grams or 4 tablespoons dried shredded coconut, unsweetened

8 grams or 1 tablespoon oat bran

7 grams or 1 tablespoon flaxseed meal

7 grams or ½ tablespoon butter (reserve for the top if desired)

3.5 grams or ¾ teaspoon Truvia (1 packet)

1 gram or ½ teaspoon cinnamon

60 grams or ½ cup 36% heavy cream

1 cup water

Pinch of salt

1. In a small pot, add all of the ingredients and use a whisk to combine very well.
2. Heat over medium-low heat until boiling. Once the mixture has boiled, remove from the heat and transfer to a serving bowl. The porridge will continue to thicken as it cools.

Cinnamon Granola

NUTRITION FACTS **Makes 4 Servings**

Recipe Yields: 2 cups

Serving Size: ½ cup

Each Serving Provides:

2.02:1 Ratio

Calories: 244

Carbohydrate: 1.85 grams

Protein: 9.16 grams

Fat: 22.22 grams

This granola is great served with diluted heavy cream to mimic milk, sprinkled over yogurt, or tossed into a zip-top baggie to take on the road as a snack. This recipe doubles easily and the cooked granola crumbles keep well stored in an airtight container.

26 grams or 2 tablespoons whole chia seeds

⅛ cup water

2 grams or ½ teaspoon pure vanilla extract

60 grams or ½ cup macadamia nuts

28 grams or 1 scoop NOW Foods' Whey Protein Isolate (scoop is provided in container)

14 grams or 2 tablespoons flaxseed meal

10 grams or 2 teaspoons Truvia

2.5 grams or 1 teaspoon cinnamon

⅛ teaspoon salt

30 grams or 2 tablespoons melted coconut oil

Additional 1 to 2 tablespoons water

1. Preheat the oven to 350°F. Line a baking sheet with parchment paper.

2. In a small bowl, combine the chia seeds, water, and vanilla extract. Stir well. Let the chia seeds absorb the water until they are very thick and gelatinous, about 5 to 15 minutes.

3. In a food processor, combine the macadamia nuts, protein powder, flaxseed meal, Truvia, cinnamon, and salt. Pulse the ingredients until the macadamia nuts have been chopped into small pieces and the mixture looks sandy.

4. Add the chia seed mixture, coconut oil, and 1 tablespoon of water to the dry ingredients in the food processor. Pulse the ingredients again until everything is well combined and the mixture is evenly moist. If the mixture looks dry, add 1 more tablespoon of water.

5. Place spoonful of the mixture onto the parchment paper. It will be very sticky! Using wet hands; evenly flatten the mixture to ¼ inch or less in thickness. Shape and appearance do not matter.

6. Bake the granola mixture for 15 minutes. After baking, remove the pan from the oven and allow the granola to cool. Break apart the cooked pieces of granola into small, ¼-inch sized crumbles. Spread the broken pieces into an even layer on the pan.

7. Return the pan to the oven for an additional 5 to 10 minutes of baking. The granola is done when it is golden brown and completely dry. Remove from the oven and allow the granola to cool completely on the pan before storing in an airtight container.

Basic Quiche

Recipe yields 2 cups egg filling

Each Serving Provides:

2.53:1 Ratio

Calories: 416

Carbohydrate: 3.34 grams

Protein: 12.20 grams

Fat: 39.25 grams

Each Serving Provides:

1.94:1 Ratio

Calories: 184

Carbohydrate: 1.20 grams

Protein: 7.40 grams

Fat: 16.63 grams

The crust is four batches of the Almond Crackers recipe found on the Charlie Foundation website and reprinted here with their permission. It will fill one 9-inch pie pan. Add up to 1 cup of cooked vegetables to this recipe for variety. The flavor combinations are endless. With or without the crust, this quiche makes a perfect lunch or light meal.

For the crust:

120 grams or 1 cup almond flour (ground from whole, blanched almonds)

80 grams or ⅔ cup whole macadamia nuts, dry roasted with salt and finely ground in a blender after measuring

60 grams or ¼ cup plus 1 tablespoon extra-virgin olive oil

60 grams or 2 large raw egg whites

Optional: ½ teaspoon salt

For the filling:

300 grams or 6 large eggs

240 grams or 1 cup 36% heavy cream

56 grams or ½ cup shredded gruyère or mild cheddar cheese

Salt to taste

1. Preheat the oven to 350°F. Lightly grease a 9-inch glass pie dish.

2. *To make the crust:* Mix all ingredients together very well. The dough will be very sticky and should hold together when pressed into a ball. Press the dough into the dish working from the center out toward the edges. If the dough is too sticky, place the entire dish, including the dough, into the freezer for 5 to 10 minutes. Use wet fingers to press the dough into an even layer all the way to the edges of the pie dish. Pierce holes in the bottom of the crust with a fork. Bake for 25 minutes or until golden brown. Set aside and allow to cool.

3. *To make the filling:* In a large bowl, combine the heavy cream, eggs, and grated cheese. Stir very well to completely combine. Season with salt.

4. Pour the egg mixture into the cooked and cooled pie shell. Bake for 20 to 30 minutes or until the edges are set but the center still jiggles. A knife inserted into the center should come out clean. Remove from the oven and allow to cool to room temperature before serving.

Breakfast Taco

NUTRITION FACTS Makes 1 Serving

Each Serving Provides:

1.51:1 Ratio

Calories: 401

Carbohydrate: 4.48 grams

Protein: 18.36 grams

Fat: 34.45 grams

A flavorful savory breakfast option.

100 grams or 2 large eggs

7 grams or ½ tablespoon butter

36 grams or 1 La Tortilla Factory Low Carb tortilla,
original size

15 grams or 1 tablespoon mayonnaise

34 grams or ¼ of an avocado, sliced thinly

3 grams or leaves from 1 to 2 sprigs of cilantro

5–6 dashes of Tabasco Green Pepper Sauce
(not included in nutrition)

Salt and pepper to taste

1. In a bowl, beat the two eggs until blended. The whites and yolks should be very well combined.

2. Melt the butter in a small 6-inch skillet over medium heat. Pour in the egg mixture. Gently cook the eggs, scraping the sides into the center until the bottom is set. Carefully flip the eggs to cook the other side, as if you are making an omelet. When eggs reach desired doneness, remove from heat and set aside.

3. While the eggs are cooking, gently warm the tortilla over a stove flame using a set of tongs. If you do not have a gas range, wrap the tortilla in a damp paper towel and microwave for 10 to 15 seconds until warm.

4. Spread the mayonnaise onto one side of the tortilla. Place the egg onto the tortilla followed by the avocado slices, cilantro, pepper sauce, and seasonings. Fold the tortilla in half and enjoy.

Breakfast Casserole

NUTRITION FACTS   **Makes 6 Servings**

Each Serving Provides:

1.58:1 Ratio

Calories: 435

Carbohydrate: 5.27 grams

Protein: 18.56 grams

Fat: 37.71 grams

Casseroles are a fantastic place to "hide" spaghetti squash. The color and flavor virtually disappear in the egg mixture. Make a batch of this recipe on the weekend, slice it into individual servings, and wrap tightly in plastic wrap. You will have a quick breakfast on hand. No cooking required for the rest of the week!

310 grams or 2 cups cooked spaghetti squash

600 grams or 12 large eggs, mixed very well

240 grams or 1 cup 36% heavy cream

113 grams or 1 cup shredded cheddar cheese

75 grams or ½ cup diced red bell pepper

56 grams or ½ stick butter, melted

Salt and pepper to taste

1. Preheat the oven to 350°F. Lightly grease a 9 × 9-inch glass baking dish.
2. In a large mixing bowl, combine all of the ingredients very well, making sure all the pieces of squash are separated and incorporated into the mixture.
3. Pour the mixture into the baking dish. Bake in the oven on the middle rack for 25 to 30 minutes or until the center is firm and completely set. Remove and allow it to cool before serving.

▶ For variety, replace the heavy cream and bell pepper with 340 grams or 12 ounces of cooked and crumbled pork sausage (sugar free and no casings), with all of the fat drippings. Add to the mixture just before baking.

Each Serving Provides (with sausage):

1.35:1 Ratio

Calories: 356

Carbohydrate: 3.60 grams

Protein: 18.39 grams

Fat: 29.74 grams

Chocolate Peanut Butter Breakfast Shake

NUTRITION FACTS **Makes 2 Servings**

Recipe Yields: 3 cups (24 ounces)

Serving Size: 1½ cups (12 ounces)

Each Serving Provides:

1:1 Ratio

Calories: 467

Carbohydrate: 5.49 grams

Protein: 30.45 grams

Fat: 35.86 grams

Not too much chocolate, not too much peanut butter, this breakfast shake will not slow you down. This light tasting protein shake is packed with protein and perfect as a meal to grab when you are on the go.

2 cups water

113 grams or ½ cup full-fat, unsweetened coconut milk

56 grams or 2 scoops NOW Foods' Whey Protein Isolate (scoop is provided)

33 grams or 2 tablespoons plus ½ teaspoon MCT oil

32 grams or 2 tablespoons peanut butter, unsweetened, peanuts only

11 grams or 2 tablespoons cacao powder

Liquid stevia drops to taste

1. Combine all ingredients in a blender. Blend starting on low speed, increasing to high for 30 seconds. The shake ingredients should be completely emulsified. Scrape the sides of the blender if needed and blend for an additional 10 seconds. Use liquid stevia drops to sweeten to your taste. Consider flavored stevia drops such as chocolate, vanilla, or toffee for additional flavor variations.

▶ Don't want to use peanut butter? Substitute with unsweetened almond butter.

Nutrition Facts (with almond butter)
Makes 2 Servings
Recipe Yields: 3 cups (24 ounces)
Serving Size: 1½ cups (12 ounces)
Each Serving Provides:
1.6:1 Ratio
Calories: 466
Carbohydrate: 4.33 grams
Protein: 30.16 grams
Fat: 36.41 grams

Green Smoothie

NUTRITION FACTS   **Makes 6 Servings**

Recipe Yields: 4½ cups (36 ounces)

Serving Size: ¾ cups (6 ounces)

Each Serving Provides:

2.45:1 Ratio

Calories: 166

Carbohydrate: 4.76 grams

Protein: 1.61 grams

Fat: 15.59 grams

Looking for a way to increase your daily intake of dark leafy greens? Try them in a smoothie! This is a very basic version that is easy to adjust by adding protein powders, different berries, or even different vegetables. A high speed blender is worth the investment if you regularly make green smoothies. It will puree the greens much smoother than a typical blender.

400 grams or 1 (13.5-ounce) can coconut milk, full-fat, unsweetened

45 grams or 2 cups chopped kale (the noncurly variety; baby kale works very well)

120 grams or 1 cup diced cucumber including peal, no seeds

136 grams or 1 avocado

61 grams or ¼ cup freshly squeezed lemon juice

61 grams or ¼ cup orange juice, unsweetened

Water

Optional: a few drops of liquid stevia to taste

1. Combine all ingredients in a blender. Blend until very smooth and completely combined. Add enough water to make 4½ cups total.

2. Pour into six half-pint Mason jars for storage. Drink the smoothie immediately or store in the refrigerator for up to one day. Stir very well before drinking. You may also freeze the smoothie in individual portions for longer storage. The smoothie is best when consumed within two weeks after being frozen.

Baked Eggs with Cream and Herbs

NUTRITION FACTS **Makes I Serving**

Serving Size: 1 ramekin

Each Serving Provides:

2.07:1 Ratio

Calories: 174

Carbohydrate: 0.91 grams

Protein: 6.77 grams

Fat: 15.87 grams

Are you looking for an elegant, simple, and delicious breakfast dish that is as easy to make for one as it is for a large crowd? Look no further! Serve this with Fiber Rolls (page 4) to dip into the creamy yolk. Consider adding finely chopped vegetables such as fresh tomatoes, bell peppers, zucchini, or fresh spinach to add variety. Fresh pesto is another way to increase the fat content and change up the flavors. Simply repeat the same process for each ramekin to make as many servings as needed.

50 grams or I large egg

7 grams or ½ tablespoon butter, room temperature

15 grams 36% heavy cream

2 grams or I teaspoon finely chopped fresh parsley

2 grams or I teaspoon thinly sliced fresh chives

Salt and pepper to taste

1. Preheat the oven to 350°F. Generously coat the bottom and sides of a 1-cup, oven-safe ramekin with ½ tablespoon butter.

2. Crack the egg into the ramekin. (If you are adding additional vegetables to the recipe, place them into the ramekin first.) Drizzle the heavy cream over the egg. Sprinkle the top of the egg with the fresh herbs, salt, and pepper.

3. Place the ramekin on a baking sheet and bake for 15 to 20 minutes or until the egg white is opaque and the yolk is just beginning to set. Let sit for an additional 5 to 10 minutes before serving in the ramekin.

Blueberry Almond Spoonbread

NUTRITION FACTS **Makes I Servings**

Serving Size: I mug

Each Serving Provides:

1.67:1 Ratio

Calories: 378

Carbohydrate: 6.05 grams

Protein: 13.82 grams

Fat: 33.14 grams

Spoonbread recipes are traditionally made from cornmeal. Almond flour has a similar grainy texture to cornmeal and makes a great low-carb substitution. Adjust the amount of water for your preference. More water will create a softer, spoonable bread pudding–like consistency while less water will produce a muffin-like result. Either way, it's delicious!

14 grams or 1 tablespoon butter	Pinch of salt
50 grams or 1 large egg	2–4 tablespoons water
28 grams or ¼ cup almond flour	20 grams or ⅛ cup fresh blueberries
7 grams or ½ tablespoon flaxseed meal	Optional: a few drops of pure vanilla or almond extract to taste
3.5 grams or ¾ teaspoon Truvia (1 packet)	

1. Place the butter in the bottom of a large mug. Microwave the butter until it is completely melted. Swirl the butter around in the mug to coat the sides almost to the top.

2. In a small bowl, combine the egg, almond flour, flaxseed meal, Truvia, salt, and water. Stir until they are completely combined. Pour any excess butter from the mug into the batter and stir. Pour the batter into the mug. Drop the blueberries into the batter, distributing them evenly.

3. Microwave the batter for one to one and a half minutes on high. Microwave ovens vary, so you may need to adjust the time to obtain the consistency you are looking for. The center of the pudding should be set. Serve the pudding in the mug immediately. It will be very hot!

SALADS, SOUPS, AND LIGHT MEALS

Caesar Salad

Spinach and Grilled Radicchio Salad with Bacon Vinaigrette

Daikon Radish and Tahini Salad

Mediterranean Tuna Salad

Flax–Hemp Crackers

Chicken Salad

Egg Salad

Creamless Creamy Chicken Soup

Easy-Does-It Soup

Butternut Squash Soup

Green Minestrone Soup

Spinach and Lemon Soup

Roasted Eggplant Dip

Olive, Basil, and Almond Tapenade

Smoked Salmon Dip

Cod Bites with Classic Tartar Sauce

Tuna Patties

Ham and Cheese Puffs

Spinach and Ricotta Filled Portabella Mushrooms

Bun-Free Cheddar Avocado Burgers

Pepperoni and Pesto Pizza

Caesar Salad

Recipe Yields: 8 cups

Serving Size: 2 cups

Each Serving Provides:

2.61:1 Ratio

Calories: 211

Carbohydrate: 2.05 grams

Protein: 5.64 grams

Fat: 20.05 grams

This classic salad is always a hit. And no need to fuss with raw egg yolks. Mayonnaise adds rich creaminess to the dressing. Try homemade Coconut Mayonnaise (page 27) in place of the processed mayonnaise.

54 grams or ¼ cup extra virgin olive oil

30 grams or 2 tablespoons lemon juice

15 grams or 1 tablespoon mayonnaise

2 grams or ¼ teaspoon anchovy paste

1 gram or ¼ teaspoon garlic powder

50 grams or ¼ cup freshly grated Parmesan cheese

325 grams or 8 cups chopped romaine lettuce (about 2–3 romaine hearts)

Fresh ground pepper to taste

1. In a large salad bowl, combine the olive oil, lemon juice, mayonnaise, anchovy paste, and garlic powder. Use a whisk to blend the ingredients together until emulsified.
2. Place the lettuce followed by the grated Parmesan on top of the dressing in the salad bowl. Season with freshly ground black pepper. The salad may sit like this, covered with plastic wrap until it is ready to be served.
3. Immediately before serving, toss the salad ingredients together until the lettuce is completely coated with the dressing and cheese.

Coconut Mayonnaise

NUTRITION FACTS **Makes 20 Servings**

Recipe Yields: 1¼ cups

Serving Size: 1 tablespoon

Each Serving Provides:

16:1 Ratio

Calories: 104

Carbohydrate: 0.13 grams

Protein: 0.57 grams

Fat: 11.24 grams

Homemade mayonnaise is easier to make than you think! Make sure to use pasteurized eggs in the shell since you will be consuming the eggs in their raw state. The coconut oil flavor is not very apparent in the mayonnaise; however, it does help make it thicker since it solidifies at room temperature. Try this in place of the processed options in any of the recipes that call for mayonnaise.

50 grams or 1 large pasteurized egg

30 grams or 2 pasteurized egg yolks

1 gram or ½ teaspoon dried mustard (powdered variety)

15 grams or 1 tablespoon lemon juice

½ teaspoon salt

pinch of white pepper

108 grams or ½ cup melted coconut oil

108 grams or ½ cup extra virgin olive oil

1. Put the eggs, mustard, lemon juice, salt, and pepper into a food processor or blender. With the processor or blender running on low speed, add the oils very slowly. Start out with drops and then work up to about a ¹⁄₁₆-inch stream. It should take about two minutes to add the oil.
2. Continue blending until there is no free standing oil.
3. Store in refrigerator in a tightly covered glass jar for up to one month.

Spinach and Grilled Radicchio Salad with Bacon Vinaigrette

NUTRITION FACTS Makes I Serving

Each Serving Provides:

1.48:1 Ratio

Calories 498

Carbohydrate: 6.09 grams

Protein: 22.69 grams

Fat: 42.61 grams

This hearty salad with rich, warm flavors is perfect during the winter months. Both the grilled radicchio and bacon vinaigrette can be served slightly warm; the spinach will wilt and soften.

60 grams or 2 cups fresh baby spinach

I serving or 2 wedges of Grilled Balsamic Radicchio (page 97)

100 grams or 2 hard-boiled eggs, cut into wedges

15 grams or I tablespoon crumbled blue cheese

14 grams or I tablespoon pine nuts

2 tablespoons Bacon Vinaigrette (page 110)

I. Arrange the spinach leaves on a dinner plate. Top the spinach with the grilled radicchio, breaking apart the radicchio leaves if desired. Finish assembling the salad by placing the eggs, blue cheese, and pine nuts onto the spinach and radicchio. Drizzle with Bacon Vinaigrette.

Daikon Radish and Tahini Salad

NUTRITION FACTS **Makes 1 Serving**

Each Serving Provides:

1.42:1 Ratio

Calories: 378

Carbohydrate: 5.93 grams

Protein: 16.41 grams

Fat: 31.82 grams

Daikon radish is a large white radish often sold broken into smaller pieces. They have a very mild radish flavor and are a great base ingredient for a winter salad. If you do not have a spiralizer, julienne the radish into very small matchsticks.

50 grams or ½ cup peeled and spiralized daikon radish

35 grams or ½ cup shredded red cabbage

35 grams or ¼ cup cooked diced chicken breast

10 grams or 1 tablespoon crushed macadamia nuts

3.75 grams or 1 tablespoon chopped cilantro, leaves and stems

2 tablespoons Tahini Dressing (page 107)

1. Place the daikon radish and cabbage on a plate. Toss to combine. Top the radish mixture with the remaining ingredients. Drizzle with Tahini Dressing.

Mediterranean Tuna Salad

NUTRITION FACTS **Makes 4 Servings**

Recipe Yields: 2 cups

Serving Size: ½ cup

Each Serving Provides:

1.87:1 Ratio

Calories: 412

Carbohydrate: 2.46 grams

Protein: 18.21 grams

Fat: 36.60 grams

This salad is a great option for lunch or an appetizer. The endive leaves make a beautiful display and are easy for guests to use for hors d'oeuvre size bites. Alternatively, you could pair the salad with Flax–Hemp Crackers (page 31).

224 grams or 2 (5 ounce) cans solid white albacore tuna packed in oil, drained

112 grams or 1 cup crumbled feta cheese

108 grams or ½ cup extra virgin olive oil

112 grams or ½ cup diced roasted red peppers

50 grams or ¼ cup quartered green olives

15 grams or ¼ cup chopped fresh parsley

15 grams or 1 tablespoon freshly squeezed lemon juice

15 grams or 1 tablespoon drained capers in brine

fresh black pepper and salt to taste

200 grams or approximately 2 endives with leaves separated

Optional: red pepper flakes to taste

1. Crumble the tuna into a mixing bowl. Add the crumbled feta cheese, olive oil, red peppers, green olives, chopped parsley, lemon juice, and capers. Stir very well to combine. Season with fresh cracked pepper and red pepper flakes if desired.

2. Taste the salad before seasoning with salt. The cheese, olives, and capers have a lot of salty flavor on their own.

3. Divide the salad into four ½-cup servings. Serve each with equal portions of the endive leaves.

Flax–Hemp Crackers

NUTRITION FACTS Makes 15 Servings

Recipe Yields: 30 crackers

Serving Size: 2 crackers

Each Serving Provides:

1.45:1 Ratio

Calories: 84

Carbohydrate: 0.47 grams

Protein: 4.43 grams

Fat: 7.11 grams

Flax–Hemp Crackers are full of natural plant-based fats! You do not need to add any oil to make this a ketogenic recipe. The fiber from the flaxseeds is released when mixed with water. This fiber is what holds the crackers together. If you do not have Penzeys' Forward Seasoning, any dried spice combination will be fine to substitute.

120 grams or 1 cup whole flaxseeds

120 grams or ½ cup water

120 grams or 1 cup hempseeds

5 grams or 4 teaspoons Penzeys' Forward Seasoning

1. Preheat the oven to 300°F. Line a baking sheet with parchment paper.

2. Mix the water and flaxseeds together. Let the mixture sit for about five minutes or until all the water is absorbed.

3. Stir the hempseeds and seasonings into the flaxseed mixture.

4. Spread the cracker mixture onto the parchment paper and pat down with a spatula until it is even and flat. The mixture should be very thin. Score the flattened mixture with the thin side of a spatula to make rectangle cracker shapes about 3-inches long by 1-inch wide.

5. Bake the crackers for about 20 minutes. They should be dry and crisp. Allow them to cool slightly before removing from the baking sheet.

6. Break the crackers apart once they are cool and store in an airtight zip-top bag or container for about one week.

Chicken Salad

NUTRITION FACTS **Makes 6 Servings**

Recipe Yields: 3 cups

Serving Size: ½ cup

Each Serving Provides:

1.06:1 Ratio

Calories: 297

Carbohydrate: 0.81 grams

Protein: 21.13 grams

Fat: 23.22 grams

The secret to making good chicken salad is mixing the ingredients together while the chicken is still slightly warm. As an extra shortcut, use two rotisserie chickens. The chicken will be the perfect temperature by the time you are home from the grocery store. Serve with a high-fat salad dressing to increase the fat if needed. Bacon Vinaigrette (page 110) goes especially well with this recipe.

400 grams or 4 cups shredded, cooked chicken breast, white meat only (discard skin and bones)

156 grams or ⅔ cup mayonnaise

25 grams or ¼ cup diced celery

15 grams or 1 tablespoon grated yellow onion

15 grams or 1 tablespoon Dijon mustard

15 grams or ¼ cup chopped fresh parsley

Salt and pepper to taste

1. In a large bowl, mix all ingredients together very well. Cover and chill for two hours before serving.

Egg Salad

NUTRITION FACTS **Makes 8 Servings**

Recipe Yields: 4 cups

Serving Size: ½ cup

Each Serving Provides:

2.29:1 Ratio

Calories: 266

Carbohydrate: 1.09 grams

Protein: 9.74 grams

Fat: 24.76 grams

Egg Salad is a lunchtime staple. It is so easy to make a large batch and keep it on hand throughout the week. Use an electric hand mixer to combine the yolks and mayonnaise; this is the secret to making extra creamy egg salad. Add additional herbs and spices to keep it from getting boring. Be adventurous and try curry powder!

600 grams or 1 dozen large eggs

176 grams or ¾ cup mayonnaise

15 grams or 1 tablespoon Dijon mustard

50 grams or ½ cup diced celery

15 grams or 1 thinly sliced scallion

Salt and pepper to taste

1. Gently place the eggs into a large pot and cover with cold water. Place the pot over high heat and bring to a boil. Once the water has reached a full boil, turn off the heat, and cover the pot with a lid. Set a timer for 10 minutes, letting the eggs sit in the hot water. After 10 minutes, pour off the hot water and fill the pot with cold tap water. Continue to add cold water until the water the eggs are sitting in remains cool. Let the eggs sit in the cold water until they are cool enough to handle, about 15 minutes. Peal the eggs, rinsing to make sure all pieces of shell are off.

2. Separate the yolks and the whites. Place the yolks into a glass bowl and add the mayonnaise, mustard, and salt. Use an electric hand mixer to combine the yolk and mayonnaise mixture until it is mostly smooth. A few small lumps are OK.

3. Chop the egg whites into small pieces. Add the chopped egg whites, celery, and scallion to the yolk mixture. Stir very well to combine the ingredients and store in a covered glass bowl.

Creamless Creamy Chicken Soup

NUTRITION FACTS   **Makes 8 Servings**

Recipe Yields: 8 cups

Serving Size: 1 cup

Each Serving Provides:

1.81:1 Ratio

Calories: 309

Carbohydrate: 4.77 grams

Protein: 25.70 grams

Fat: 55.19 grams

Rich and creamy, yet not a drop of cream! Macadamia nuts are a versatile ingredient and this soup highlights their usefulness as a thickening agent. If the soup becomes too thick after it is pureed, add a little more water to thin to your liking. Try substituting the Swanson Chicken Broth with my Homemade Chicken Broth (page 35) and adjust the nutritional information accordingly.

108 grams or ½ cup olive oil

40 grams or ¼ cup finely diced yellow onion

64 grams or ½ cup diced carrots

100 grams or 1 cup sliced celery

946 grams or 1 quart Swanson Chicken Broth, 100% Natural

132 grams or 1 cup macadamia nuts

1 cup water

280 grams or 2 cups diced cooked chicken breast

Optional: salt and pepper to taste

Optional: Herbs de Provence or Italian herbs to taste

1. Heat the olive oil in a large pot over medium heat. Add the onion, carrots, and celery. Sauté the vegetables, until the onion is translucent.

2. Add the broth and macadamia nuts. Heat until the soup reaches a simmer then reduce the heat to maintain a slow simmer. Simmer for 20 to 30 minutes or until the vegetables are tender.

3. Pour the soup into a blender. Make sure the steam can escape from the blender by removing the center of the lid or by leaving it slightly ajar. Cover the lid with a towel to prevent splattering and blend until the macadamia nuts are completely pureed. Pour the pureed soup back into the pot.

4. Pour 1 cup of water into the blender and run the blender for a few seconds until all the soup clinging to the sides has been combined with the water. Add the water to the soup to thin the consistency.

5. Add the diced chicken to the soup and season to your liking. Heat just until hot then serve.

Homemade Chicken Broth

NUTRITION FACTS (homemade) Makes 16 Servings

Recipe Yields: 1 gallon

Serving Size: 1 cup

Each Serving Provides:

0.46: 1 Ratio

Calories: 17

Carbohydrate: 0.88 grams

Protein: 1.19 grams

Fat: 0.95 grams

NUTRITION FACTS (Swanson Chicken Broth, 100% natural)

Serving Size: 1 cup

Each Serving Provides:

0.25:1 Ratio

Calories 12

Carbohydrate: 0.99 grams

Protein: 0.99 grams

Fat: 0.49 grams

Homemade Chicken Broth is always better than store-bought prepared broth. You can be assured when you make your own broth there will be no additives, preservatives, or artificial colorings. Broth is easy to make and saves a lot of money as well. All the recipes in this cookbook have been calculated with Swanson Chicken Broth, 100% Natural. If you use the homemade broth recipe, carbohydrate will be slightly reduced; fat and protein will slightly increase. We have provided nutrition information for both homemade and Swanson's so you can compare.

Leftover bones and meat of one roasted chicken (organic preferred)

4 stalks of celery, cut in half

2 carrots, cut into 1-inch pieces

1 small yellow onion (or half of a large onion), cut in half or quarters

2 sprigs of fresh parsley

1 3-inch sprig of fresh rosemary

1 3-inch sprig of fresh thyme

2 bay leaves

1 teaspoon salt

1 tablespoon apple cider vinegar (does not contribute any flavor, but helps draw minerals from the chicken bones)

1 gallon cold filtered water

1. All ingredients should be cold, including the chicken. Put all of the ingredients into a large stockpot. Make sure the pot is large enough to accommodate all of the water.

2. Bring the pot to a boil. As soon as it boils, turn the heat down to a very low simmer.

3. Simmer the broth for two hours; skim the top occasionally if foam appears.

4. After two hours, allow the broth to cool slightly before refrigerating. Refrigerate the broth until completely cool.

5. Once the broth is completely cool, strain it very well. Remove all of the ingredients including any fat that has congealed on the top.

6. Store in the refrigerator for about one week or freeze in small portions.

Easy-Does-It Soup

NUTRITION FACTS Makes 4 Servings

Recipe Yields: 4 cups

Serving Size: I cup

Each Serving Provides:

1.84:I Ratio

Calories: 286 calories

Carbohydrate: 6.85 grams

Protein: 7.05 grams

Fat: 25.60 grams

Are you recovering from an illness? This recipe is for you! Packed with nutrients, this soup is designed to be easily digestible and free of any ingredients that may not agree with a sensitive stomach. Try substituting the Swanson Chicken Broth with my Homemade Chicken Broth (page 35) and adjust the nutritional information accordingly.

946 grams or I quart Swanson Chicken Broth, 100% Natural

140 grams or I cup peeled and cubed butternut squash

55 grams or ¼ cup ghee

50 grams or ½ cup sliced celery

40 grams or ¼ cup diced onion

56 grams or ¼ cup coconut milk, full-fat and unsweetened

136 grams or 8 egg yolks (discard whites)

Salt to taste

1. Combine the chicken broth, butternut squash, ghee, celery, onion, and coconut milk in a pot set over medium heat. Bring the soup to a simmer. Simmer for about 30 minutes or until the squash is tender and easily pierced with a fork.

2. Transfer the soup to a blender. Place the lid on the blender, removing the center of the lid to allow steam to escape. Alternatively, leave the lid slightly ajar, cover the lid with a clean towel to prevent splattering, and puree until completely combined. Return the soup to the pot and set over low heat.

3. Place egg yolks into a large bowl. Add ¼ cup of the soup to the egg yolks and whisk to combine. Add an additional ¼ cup of the soup to the egg yolks and whisk again to combine.

4. Pour the tempered egg yolks into the pot of soup, stirring very well to combine. Stir constantly while heating the soup until it reaches 140°F. This should only take about five minutes. Pour into Mason jars to freeze or serve immediately.

Butternut Squash Soup

NUTRITION FACTS   **Makes 8 Servings**

Serving Size: ¾ cup

Each Serving Provides:

1.67:1 Ratio

Calories: 162

Carbohydrate: 6.98 grams

Protein: 1.54 grams

Fat: 14.19 grams

No need for a long list of ingredients or spices to make a delicious butternut squash soup! This simple recipe always produces a delicious and satisfying soup. You can easily change the flavor of the soup with herbs and spices. Thyme, curry powder, chili flakes, or ground sumac will enhance the savory flavors while warming spices, such as cinnamon, nutmeg, and allspice will produce a sweeter result. Freeze ¾ cup portions in Mason jars and season them after thawing for a different take on the soup every time you eat it!

Try substituting the Swanson Chicken Broth with my Homemade Chicken Broth (page 35) and adjust the nutritional information accordingly.

69 grams or ¼ cup plus 1 tablespoon olive oil (divided)

454 grams or 1 pound butternut squash (about ½ of a squash), peeled, deseeded, and chopped into 1-inch pieces

9 grams or 3 teaspoons minced fresh garlic (about 3 cloves)

946 grams or 1 quart Swanson Chicken Broth, 100% Natural

2 bay leaves

120 grams or ½ cup 36% heavy cream, reserve some for the top if desired

1 teaspoon sea salt

1. Heat 1 tablespoon of olive oil in a heavy pot over medium heat. Add the butternut squash, garlic, and salt. Sauté until the garlic begins to turn golden brown, about three to five minutes.

2. Add the chicken broth, ¼ cup of olive oil, and bay leaves to the butternut squash. Bring the mixture to a boil. Once boiling, reduce to a simmer and cook for about 30 minutes or until the squash is completely cooked through and can be easily pierced with a fork.

3. Remove the bay leaves from the soup and transfer the soup to a blender. Do not fill the blender more than three-quarters full! Make sure the steam can escape from the blender by removing the center of the lid or by leaving it slightly ajar. Cover the lid with a towel to prevent splattering and blend until the soup is pureed. Alternatively, use an immersion blender and puree the soup in the cooking pot.

4. While the blender is running, pour in the cream. Finish the soup by adding the sea salt and any additional herbs and spices of your choice. Store extra servings in Mason jars and freeze.

Green Minestrone Soup

NUTRITION FACTS **Makes 4 Servings**

Recipe Yields: 4 cups

Serving Size: 1 cup

Each Serving Provides:

2.08:1 Ratio

Calories: 157

Carbohydrate: 4.47 grams

Protein: 2.42 grams

Fat: 14.33 grams

You guessed it, just about everything in this soup is green! All of the ingredients are very low carb making for a generous-sized portion to enjoy. Try substituting the Swanson Chicken Broth with my Homemade Chicken Broth (page 35), and adjust the nutritional information accordingly.

54 grams or ¼ cup olive oil

250 grams or 2 cups ½-inch diced zucchini (about 2 small zucchini)

100 grams or 1 cup sliced celery stalks

50 grams or 2 cups torn 1-inch kale pieces (curly variety)

40 grams or ¼ cup diced yellow onion

3 grams or 1 teaspoon minced garlic

946 grams or 1 quart Swanson Chicken Broth, 100% Natural

Salt and pepper to taste

1. Heat the olive oil in a large pot over medium high heat. Add all of the vegetables to the olive oil and sauté until the kale pieces are wilted. Pour the chicken broth over the vegetables and bring to a simmer. Simmer for 30 minutes or until all of the vegetables are tender and easily pierced with a fork. Season with salt and pepper to taste and serve hot.

▶ *For a slightly thicker soup*: Remove 1 cup of the cooked soup and use an immersion blender to completely puree it. Return the pureed soup to the pot and stir well to combine. This will intensify the green color and give a little more body to the soup.

Spinach and Lemon Soup

NUTRITION FACTS **Makes 6 Servings**

Recipe Yields: 6 cups

Serving Size: 1 cup

Each Serving Provides:

1.98:1 Ratio

Calories: 312

Carbohydrate: 3.90 grams

Protein: 10.36 grams

Fat: 28.30 grams

Mature spinach is a great choice to use in soup. It is the least expensive fresh spinach you can buy and it is slightly heartier than baby spinach so it won't disappear when added to the soup. Make sure you wash the spinach very well, fully submerging the leaves in cold water and allowing it to sit for about five minutes so that all of the sand sinks to the bottom. Try substituting the Swanson Chicken Broth with my Homemade Chicken Broth (page 35) and adjust the nutritional information accordingly.

40 grams or ¼ cup diced yellow onion

84 grams or ¼ cup plus 2 tablespoons olive oil (divided)

227 grams or ½ pound chopped fresh spinach including stems

6 grams or 2 teaspoons minced garlic

946 grams or 1 quart Swanson Chicken Broth, 100% Natural

61 grams or ¼ cup freshly squeezed lemon juice

113 grams or ½ cup coconut milk, full-fat and unsweetened

135 grams or 1 cup hempseeds

Salt and pepper to taste

Optional: chopped fresh dill to taste

1. Heat ¼ cup of olive oil in a pot over medium heat. Add the onion and sauté until soft. Add the chopped spinach and garlic and cook until the spinach is wilted but still bright green.

2. Add the chicken broth, lemon juice, and coconut milk and the remaining 2 tablespoons of the olive oil. Heat the soup until it reaches a full simmer and the spinach stems are tender, about five minutes.

3. Add the hempseeds, season to taste, and stir to evenly combine. Serve immediately or, once cooled, freeze in 1 cup portions.

Roasted Eggplant Dip

NUTRITION FACTS   **Makes 16 Servings**

Recipe Yields: 2 cups

Serving Size: 2 tablespoons

Each Serving Provides:

2.19:1 Ratio

Calories: 68

Carbohydrate: 1.80 grams

Protein: 1.05 grams

Fat: 6.26 grams

Serve this dip with Fiber Roll crackers (page 4) or use as a spread in a low-carb wrap. This is a great complement to any protein, especially grilled chicken or steak.

908 grams or 2 eggplants, about 1 pound each

85 grams or ⅓ cup chopped roasted red peppers

72 grams or ⅓ cup extra virgin olive oil

37 grams or ⅓ cup pine nuts

30 grams or 2 tablespoons freshly squeezed lemon juice

17 grams or 1 tablespoon crumbled feta cheese

Salt and pepper to taste

Optional: garlic powder to taste

Optional: fresh oregano to taste, reserve some to sprinkle on top

1. Preheat the oven to 400°F. Slice the eggplants in half lengthwise. Place them on a foil lined rimmed baking sheet. Roast them uncovered for about one hour or until eggplants are very soft.

2. Set eggplants aside until they are cool enough to handle. Scrape all of the cooked flesh out of the eggplant skins and place in a food processor. Discard the skins.

3. To the food processor, add red peppers, olive oil, pine nuts, and lemon juice. Puree the mixture until smooth. Season with salt and pepper and add additional seasonings to your liking.

4. Transfer the dip to a serving bowl and top with crumbled feta cheese and reserved oregano.

Olive, Basil, and Almond Tapenade

NUTRITION FACTS Makes 15 Servings

Recipe Yields: 1.875 cups

Serving Size: 2 tablespoons

Each Serving Provides:

6.42:1 Ratio

Calories: 114

Carbohydrate: 0.64 grams

Protein: 1.21 grams

Fat: 11.87 grams

Although tapenade is typically used as a spread or a dip, try using this as a topping for grilled meats. It is an easy way to wake up plain chicken or add flavor to a mild white fish.

224 grams or 2 cups pitted green olives

72 grams or ½ cup slivered almonds

1.5 grams or ½ teaspoon minced fresh garlic

15 grams or 1 tablespoon lemon juice

5 grams or 1 teaspoon drained capers in brine

8 grams or ½ cup loosely packed fresh basil leaves

108 grams or ½ cup extra virgin olive oil

Pinch of salt

1. Place the olives, almonds, garlic, lemon juice, and capers in the bowl of a food processor.

2. Coarsely chop the basil leaves then add them to the food processor and pulse a few times.

3. Add the olive oil and a pinch of salt. Pulse the food processor until mixture forms a coarse paste but still has texture.

4. Transfer to a bowl, cover, and refrigerate until ready to serve. This will keep in the refrigerator for about three to five days.

Smoked Salmon Dip

NUTRITION FACTS Makes 16 Servings

Recipe Yields: 2 cups

Serving Size: 2 tablespoons

Each Serving Provides:

2.25:1 Ratio

Calories: 99

Carbohydrate: 0.42 grams

Protein: 3.67 grams

Fat: 9.21 grams

Spread this on crackers for a savory breakfast that mimics lox and cream cheese on a bagel, but without all the carbs of course!

227 grams or 1 (8 ounce) package smoked salmon

227 grams or 1 (8 ounce) package full-fat cream cheese, room temperature

73 grams or ⅓ cup mayonnaise

2.5 grams or ⅛ cup chopped fresh dill

Salt and pepper to taste

Optional: sprinkle of coarse grey sea salt

1. Combine the smoked salmon, cream cheese, and mayonnaise in a food processor. Process until all ingredients are evenly combined.
2. Spread the dip onto a serving plate and top with the fresh dill, salt, and pepper.
3. Coarse grey sea salt is recommended to sprinkle on top.

Cod Bites with Classic Tartar Sauce

A kid and grownup favorite! This method of breading is simpler than traditional breading methods. You will have this in the oven in no time.

680 grams or 12 ounces pacific cod filets, skinned and deboned

15 grams or 1 tablespoon raw egg white (about ½ of one large egg white)

15 grams or 1 tablespoon extra virgin olive oil

36 grams or ⅓ cup Quick and Easy Low-Carb Bread Crumbs (page 46)

Salt and pepper to taste

1 batch or 1 cup of Classic Tartar Sauce (page 117)

1. Preheat the oven to 425°F. Line a baking sheet with parchment paper.

2. Cut the cod filets into 1-inch pieces. Use a paper towel to dry the fish very well. Place the pieces of cod onto a plate. Pour the egg white, olive oil, and seasonings on to the fish. Use your hands to toss the cod pieces to evenly coat with the wet ingredients. Sprinkle the bread crumbs over the cod. Again, toss to evenly coat all the pieces. This is a thin coating.

3. Arrange the cod pieces on the baking sheet so they are not touching. Make sure all of the coating has been used. Bake for 20 to 30 minutes or until the fish is completely cooked through. The flesh should be opaque white and flake easily. Divide the cod bites into four equal portions and serve with ¼ cup of Tartar Sauce.

Quick and Easy Low-Carb Bread Crumbs

NUTRITION FACTS Makes 1 Serving

Recipe Yields: ⅓ cup

Serving Size: ⅓ cup

Each Serving Provides:

0.25:1 Ratio

Calories: 50 calories

Carbohydrate: 3.00 grams

Protein: 5.00 grams

Fat: 2.00 grams

This is a shortcut trick that is super easy and fast. This is one prepared item that is worth the extra cost for the convenience they provide. La Tortilla Factory brand is found in most grocery stores in the United States. There are two sizes of low-carb tortillas, always by the smaller size. The serving size should be listed on the package as "1 Tortilla (36 g)."

1 Package La Tortilla Factory, High Fiber, Low Carb Tortillas

1. Tear the tortillas into large pieces.
2. Use a high speed blender or food processor with a chopping blade. Blend or pulse the tortilla pieces until they are ground into fine bread crumbs. Only blend one to two tortillas at a time. Make sure there are no large pieces remaining.
3. Store in an airtight container. Freeze for longer storage.

Tuna Patties

NUTRITION FACTS **Makes 4 Servings**

Serving Size: 1 patty

Each Serving Provides:

2.01:1 Ratio

Calories: 324

Carbohydrate: 0.90 grams

Protein: 13.72 grams

Fat: 29.45 grams

It you're tired of tuna salad, here's another quick, simple way to enjoy tuna.

224 grams or 2 (5-ounce) cans chunk light tuna in water, drained

50 grams or 1 large egg

30 grams or 2 tablespoons mayonnaise

28 grams or ¼ cup almond flour

27 grams or ⅛ cup extra virgin olive oil

56 grams or ½ stick butter

Salt and pepper to taste

1. Make sure the tuna is drained very well. Combine the tuna, egg, mayonnaise, almond flour, olive oil, salt, and pepper in a bowl. Stir to combine very well.

2. In a 12-inch square nonstick skillet, melt the butter over medium heat. Drop a quarter of the tuna mixture into the melted butter and form a patty about 5 inches in diameter. Make three more patties with the remaining mixture.

3. Fry the patties on one side for about three to four minutes. When the edges begin to brown, flip the patties to cook the other side for three to four minutes or until the patties are set around the edges.

4. Lower the heat to a low setting and continue to cook the patties until the center is firm and most of the butter has been absorbed. You may flip the tuna patties several more times to help the butter fully absorb.

5. Once the patties have cooked through, turn the heat off and allow the patties to finish absorbing all of the remaining butter. The patties should be brown and crispy. Serve immediately.

Ham and Cheese Puffs

NUTRITION FACTS *Makes 6 Servings*

Recipe Yields: 12 puffs

Serving Size: 2 puffs

Each Serving Provides:

1:82 Ratio

Calories: 399

Carbohydrate: 3.08 grams

Protein: 16.49 grams

Fat: 35.64 grams

One way to make a meal more versatile or interesting is to try alternative cooking methods. Although the title of this recipe is Ham and Cheese Puffs, don't let that limit you to only making these in a doughnut hole–shaped pan. A muffin tin and liners work perfectly. If you have nonstick pans in other shapes or countertop cooking appliances, such as a mini doughnut pan or a waffle maker, try a batch in each. Fun shapes keep things interesting!

200 grams 4 large eggs

118 grams or ½ cup mayonnaise

54 grams or ¼ cup coconut oil

56 grams or ¼ cup coconut flour

1 gram or ¼ teaspoon baking powder

1 gram or ¼ teaspoon baking soda

198 grams or 7 ounces sliced plain deli ham, diced very small

113 grams or 1 cup shredded cheddar cheese

1. Preheat the oven to 350°F. Lightly grease a nonstick doughnut hole–shaped pan.

2. In a mixing bowl, whisk together the eggs, mayonnaise, and coconut oil.

3. Stir in the coconut flour, baking powder, and baking soda to the wet ingredients.

4. Fold the ham and the cheese into the batter, making sure to break up any lumps. Fill the wells about three-quarters full with the batter. Bake for 20 to 30 minutes. The puffs should be a light golden brown and dry throughout.

Spinach and Ricotta Filled Portabella Mushrooms

NUTRITION FACTS   **Makes 4 Servings**

Each Serving Provides:

1:39 Ratio

357 calories

Carbohydrate: 5.65 grams

Protein: 15.90 grams

Fat: 30.05 grams

Portabella mushrooms make a very satisfying meat-free meal. They are also conveniently sized for individual portions. Choose mushrooms that have a deep rim as it will help contain the filling. Try other dark leafy greens besides spinach in this recipe. Kale, swiss chard, or even dandelion greens would taste great as well. It is easier to fill the mushrooms with greens that have already been wilted. Simply sauté fresh greens or use frozen greens that have been thawed and well drained.

454 grams 1 pound portabella mushroom caps (about 4 large)

142 grams or ½ cup drained and packed cooked spinach

213 grams or ¾ cup full-fat ricotta cheese

72 grams or ⅓ cup extra virgin olive oil

50 grams or ½ cup grated Parmesan cheese

50 grams or 1 large egg

3 grams or 1 teaspoon minced garlic

Salt and pepper to taste

1. Preheat the oven to 425°F and line a baking sheet with aluminum foil.

2. Clean the mushroom caps by brushing any dirt off with a pastry brush. Remove the stem and scrape the dark gills out with a spoon. Be careful to leave the edge of the mushroom intact. Season the inside of the mushrooms with salt and pepper. Bake these for about 15 minutes while you prepare the filling. This gives the thick mushrooms a head start in the baking process. Alternatively, you can grill these to add additional smoky and charred flavor.

3. Combine the remaining ingredients and stir very well. Fill each prebaked mushroom cap with one-quarter of the filling mixture. Return the baking sheet to the oven and bake for 25 to 30 minutes. The tops should be slightly browned and the mushroom caps should be tender. Allow to cool for 5 to 10 minutes before serving.

Bun-Free Cheddar Avocado Burgers

Recipe Yields: 4 patties

Serving Size: 1 patty

Each Serving Provides:

1:09 Ratio

Calories: 409 calories

Carbohydrate: 0.91 grams

Protein: 28.77 grams

Fat: 32.27 grams

This simple combination of ingredients is a personal family favorite reserved for busy weeknights, camping, and even eating out. On a busy weeknight, throw the patties in the oven and dinner is ready in 20 minutes. At cookouts, it's a no-brainer meal that still lets you partake in the food being served. It is usually possible to order this from a restaurant menu after confirming there are no fillers in the meat.

454 grams or 1 pound 85% lean ground beef

136 grams or 1 avocado

112 grams or 4 (1-ounce) slices yellow cheddar cheese

Salt and pepper

1. Make four burger patties from the ground beef. Use a burger patty press for consistent sizes and shapes. The patties will shrink when cooked, so make them wider than you want the cooked burger to be. Season the patties with salt and pepper.

2. Grill or broil the burger patties until they are cooked to your liking. Transfer the cooked patties to a plate. Lay a quarter of the avocado slices on each patty. Cover the avocado with a slice of cheese. Use a second plate or a piece of foil to cover the patties; this will allow the residual heat to melt the cheese. Once the cheese is melted, serve the burgers with a side of your choice.

Pepperoni and Pesto Pizza

NUTRITION FACTS **Makes 2 Servings**

Recipe Yields: 2 pizzas

Serving Size: 1 pizza

Each Serving Provides:

2.04:1 Ratio

Calories: 586

Carbohydrate: 5.60 grams

Protein: 20.59 grams

Fat: 53.38 grams

The best way to make this pizza is to put the toppings on the dough before baking. This way, the toppings will not make the pizza soggy, nor will they slide off creating a very messy eating experience. Once the pizzas are baked, they are ready to be frozen. They keep very well in the freezer for up to two months. Let the pizzas cool, then wrap tightly in plastic wrap. To reheat, bake in a 350°F oven for 10 to 15 minutes or microwave for two to three minutes. For a crispier crust, heat the pizza in a nonstick skillet covered with a lid over low-medium heat. The toppings will melt while the bottom of the crust crisps up.

One batch Fiber Rolls dough (page 4)

4 tablespoons Kale Pesto (page 116)

56 grams or 2 ounces sliced fresh mozzarella (about ¼ cup)

28 grams or 1 ounce sliced pepperoni (about 16 slices)

1. Preheat the oven to 450°F. Line a baking sheet with aluminum foil. Generously grease the foil. A nonstick baking mat may also be used. Parchment paper should be avoided, as it tends to burn.

2. Divide the Fiber Rolls dough in half. Put each half on the baking sheet and use wet hands to press into a flat circle about 8 to 9 inches across.

3. Spread 2 tablespoons of the Kale Pesto onto each pizza round. Top each pizza with half of the pepperoni and mozzarella. Bake for 30 minutes in the bottom third of the oven.

4. After baking, let the pizza cool for about five minutes. If the oil from the pesto has seeped over the sides of the pizza, it will reabsorb while cooling. Slice each pizza into four pieces and serve.

DINNER

Classic Beef Chili

Cheesesteak Plate

Miso Beef

Beef and Mushroom Stew

Braciole in Tomato Broth

Chicken Peanut Curry

Buffalo Chicken Meatballs

Creamy Balsamic Chicken

Chicken Piccata

Chicken Enchiladas

Moussaka

Pork Tenderloin with Dijon Sauce and Rutabaga Noodles

Pork Carnitas with Chimichurri Sauce

Stuffed Poblano Peppers

Vegan Taco Salad

Egg and Cauliflower Fried Rice

Baked Cod with Roasted Red Pepper Sauce

Coconut Shrimp with Peanut Sauce

Deviled Clams

Sriracha Scallop Roll

Classic Beef Chili

NUTRITION FACTS   **Makes 6 Servings**

Recipe Yields: 3 cups

Serving Size: ½ cup

Each Serving Provides:

1.2:1 Ratio

Calories: 532

Carbohydrate: 3.65 grams

Protein: 32.31 grams

Fat: 43.15 grams

Traditional beef chili does not contain tomato or beans, both of which are carbohydrates. This works in favor for creating a ketogenic chili recipe! It is easy to customize this recipe by using different types of chili powder. Just make sure the blend you use is 100% dried chilies. Seasoning packets will often contain cornstarch, sugar, and other additives.

Chili is always better eaten the next day. This recipe calls for a lot of broth, which will be reduced by half during the cooking process. This helps deepen the flavors of the dish and will allow the meat to become very tender.

To increase the fat content further, add a full-fat topping such as sour cream or avocado.

908 grams or 2 pounds 85% raw ground beef

120 grams or ¾ cup diced yellow onion

16 grams or 2 tablespoons chili powder

2 grams or 1 teaspoon cumin seeds

2 grams or 2 teaspoons dried oregano

1.5 grams or ½ teaspoon garlic powder

1,892 grams or 2 quarts beef broth

108 grams or ½ cup extra virgin olive oil

28 grams or 4 tablespoons flaxseed meal

Salt and pepper to taste

1. Heat a large Dutch oven or other heavy bottomed pot over high heat. Add the beef, onion, chili powder, cumin seeds, oregano, and garlic powder to the pot. Sauté the ingredients until the beef is cooked thoroughly with no pink remaining. Do not drain any fat from the beef!

2. Add the beef broth, olive oil, and flaxseed meal to the beef mixture. Bring to a full boil. Reduce the heat to medium high so the chili maintains a very high simmer. Simmer the chili uncovered, stirring occasionally for up to two hours or until the broth has reduced by half. The chili will have thickened and all ingredients should be evenly suspended in the mixture.

3. Let the chili rest overnight in the refrigerator. Reheat over medium heat prior to serving. Season with salt and pepper and enjoy.

Cheesesteak Plate

NUTRITION FACTS Makes 6 servings

Each Serving Provides:

1:64 Ratio

Calories: 557 calories

Carbohydrate: 4.78 grams

Protein: 24.94 grams

Fat: 48.68 grams

Who doesn't love the flavors of a cheesesteak? This recipe is bread free, but all the flavors are still there to enjoy. Try this with a side serving of Fiber Rolls (page 4) if you must have bread.

454 grams or 1 pound shaved beefsteak

115 grams or 1¼ cup sliced red bell pepper

115 grams or 1¼ cup sliced yellow bell pepper

115 grams or 1¼ cup sliced green bell pepper

58 grams or ½ cup sliced onion

15 grams or 1 tablespoon coconut oil

1 batch or 2 cups Cheese Sauce (page 103)

Salt and pepper to taste

1. Heat coconut oil in a large nonstick skillet over high heat. Add bell peppers and onion. Sauté the peppers and onion until they have softened. Be careful not to overcook until they are mushy. Remove the peppers and onion from the pan and set aside.

2. Add the beef to the pan in an even, thin layer. Cook the meat until it is no longer pink. Lightly season with salt and pepper.

3. Add the peppers and onion back to the pan with the meat. Toss the ingredients until equally distributed. Divide into six equal servings. Place each serving on a serving plate and top with ⅓ cup of cheese sauce. Serve and enjoy.

Miso Beef

NUTRITION FACTS **Makes 4 servings**

Each Serving Provides:

1:1 Ratio

Calories: 373

Carbohydrate: 2.60 grams

Protein: 25.86 grams

Fat: 28.76 grams

Miso paste is a Japanese seasoning made from fermented soybeans. It is fantastic when combined with meats and vegetables. There are several varieties to choose from; white miso is the mildest in flavor. Miso contains a lot of salt, so be cautious when seasoning with additional salt.

85 grams or ¾ stick butter, room temperature

18 grams or 3 teaspoons white miso paste

454 grams or 1 pound flank steak

454 grams or 1 pound spiral or matchstick-sliced fresh zucchini (about 4–5 small ones)

¼ cup water

7 grams or ½ tablespoon toasted sesame oil

Salt and pepper to taste

1. Mix the butter and miso paste together until completely combined. Cover and set aside.
2. Season the flank steak with salt and pepper. Grill the flank steak on a gas or charcoal grill. Cook until the meat has reached 160°F or medium well-done with a slightly pink center. Remove the meat from the grill and cover with foil. Allow it to rest for 15 minutes.
3. Place the zucchini in a glass bowl and add ¼ cup water. Cover the bowl with a plate and steam in a microwave for two to three minutes or until the zucchini is bright green and slightly softened. Drain excess water and toss the zucchini with the sesame oil.
4. To serve, slice the steak across the grain into very thin slices. Divide steak and zucchini into four equal portions. Place steak on top of zucchini and top with one-quarter of the butter mixture (about 1½ tablespoons).

Beef and Mushroom Stew

NUTRITION FACTS   **Makes 4 Servings**

Each Serving Provides:

1:76 Ratio

Calories: 648

Carbohydrate: 5.91 grams

Protein: 26.67 grams

Fat: 57.43 grams

What could be better on a cold winter night than a rich and earthy beef stew? This is the kind of recipe that makes your entire house smell great. It is especially good served as leftovers.

108 grams or ½ cup extra virgin olive oil

56 grams or ½ stick butter

454 grams or 1 pound 1-inch cubed stew meat

454 grams or 1 pound (two 8-ounce containers) sliced baby portabella mushrooms

80 grams or ½ cup diced onion

946 grams or 1 quart beef broth

15 grams or 1 tablespoon flaxseed meal

3 grams or 1 teaspoon minced garlic

1 gram or 1 teaspoon dried thyme

2 bay leaves

15 grams or ¼ cup chopped fresh parsley

Salt and pepper to taste

1. Heat the butter and olive oil in a large heavy pot over medium to high heat until the butter is completely melted. Add the meat and sauté until all sides have browned.

2. Add the mushrooms and onion. Sauté until the mushrooms are soft. Add the broth, flaxseed meal, garlic, thyme, and bay leaves. Simmer on low to medium for at least two hours or until the meat is very tender.

3. Remove the bay leaves. Using two forks shred the chunks of meat before serving. Add the fresh parsley and stir well. Divide into four portions and enjoy.

Braciole in Tomato Broth

NUTRITION FACTS **Makes 4 Servings**

Each Serving Provides:

1:49 Ratio

Calories: 710

Carbohydrate: 7.44 grams

Protein: 33.38 grams

Fat: 60.70 grams

A favorite Sunday meal with a keto twist. Adding beef broth to the tomato sauce cuts down on carbs but amps up the flavor. Some of the filling will cook out of the meat. Just stir this into the sauce for added flavor. Most flank steaks are about 2 pounds. If that is the case, simply double the recipe and serve to guests or save the extra for leftovers. Be sure to have several feet of butcher twine cut and ready.

454 grams or 1 pound flank steak

56 grams or ½ stick butter, room temperature

56 grams or ½ cup pine nuts

50 grams or ½ cup grated Parmesan cheese

36 grams or ⅓ cup Quick and Easy Low-Carb Bread Crumbs (page 46)

15 grams or ¼ cup chopped fresh parsley

6 grams or 2 teaspoons minced garlic

⅛ teaspoon xanthan gum (helps keep ingredients emulsified)

108 grams or ½ cup olive oil

40 grams or ¼ cup diced yellow onion

411 grams or 1 (14.5 ounce) can beef broth (almost 2 cups)

250 grams or 1 cup pureed canned tomatoes

4 grams or 1 tablespoon dried Italian herb blend

Salt and pepper to taste

1. Lay the flank steak on a cutting board with the grain of the meat running vertically (up and down) to you. With a very sharp knife (and possibly protective gloves), butterfly the steak along the grain of the meat. Make small slices working from top to bottom, repeating until you have sliced through the entire steak. Stop slicing just before you reach the other side. Be very careful to not slice any areas too thin so that you create holes as this will let the filling seep out. Fold the steak open. It should now open like an open book and have doubled in size. Use a meat pounder (or rolling pin) to gently pound any areas that are thicker so you have one even piece of meat. Or skip all this and ask a butcher to do it for you!

2. In a food processor, combine the butter, pine nuts, Parmesan cheese, bread crumbs, parsley, garlic, and xanthan gum. Season with salt and pepper. Run the processor until all ingredients are evenly combined. The texture can be as chunky or smooth as you would like.

3. Turn the steak so the grain of the meat is now running horizontal (side-to-side) to you. Make sure it is folded open. Have several feet of butcher twine cut and ready. Spread the bread crumb mixture in an even layer over the bottom two-thirds of the meat. Be careful not to spread it all the way to the edges as the meat will shrink once it is cooked. Starting at the bottom, roll the meat into a tight log. Continue rolling until it is completely rolled. Tie the meat with the twine every 2 inches, making sure the ends are very tightly tied. Be careful not to squeeze out the filling.

4. Heat a large deep-sided pan or oval Dutch oven over medium heat. The pan should be large enough to fit the rolled up flank steak. Add the oil and onion to the pan and sauté for about five minutes or until the onion is translucent. Place the flank steak into the pan seam side down and brown each side. Carefully turn the meat with a set of tongs. Do not pierce the meat.

5. Once all sides of the meat have been browned, add the beef broth, tomato puree, and dried herbs. Season the sauce with salt. Bring the tomato broth to a boil and then reduce the heat to maintain a simmer. Cover the pan with a lid, leaving the lid slightly ajar, and simmer for one and a half hours, turning the steak every 15 to 20 minutes. Stir the sauce very well each time you turn the meat. The flank steak should reach an internal temperature of 170°F. Allow the steak to rest in the pan with the heat off for about 30 minutes prior to slicing.

6. To slice the meat, remove it from the pan onto a cutting board. With a very sharp knife, slice it into eight rounds. If you have rolled the meat properly, you will now be slicing it against the grain creating very tender pieces. If you rolled it the wrong way, you will have very long strands of chewy meat. Some of the filling will seep out as you are cutting it. Just do your best to divide it equally onto each piece.

7. To plate, pour a quarter of the remaining sauce onto a plate and top with two slices of meat.

Chicken Peanut Curry

NUTRITION FACTS (with cauliflower) **Makes 6 Servings**

Each Serving Provides:

1:21 Ratio

Calories: 417

Carbohydrate: 6.37 grams

Protein: 21.56 grams

Fat: 33.89 grams

NUTRITION FACTS (without cauliflower) **Makes 6 Servings**

Each Serving Provides:

1:38 Ratio

Calories: 398

Carbohydrate: 4.56 grams

Protein: 19.72 grams

Fat: 33.44 grams

Curry hits the spot when you have a craving for takeout. Once you have the ingredients ready, the dish comes together very quickly! This recipe calls for sliced chicken breast. Try freezing thinly sliced chicken breast to help the recipe come together even faster.

45 grams or 3 tablespoons melted coconut oil

45 grams or 3 tablespoons melted palm oil

80 grams or ½ cup diced yellow onion

6 grams or 1 tablespoon curry powder

454 grams or 1 pound thinly sliced chicken breast

6 grams or 2 teaspoons minced garlic

6 grams or 2 teaspoons minced fresh ginger root

400 grams or 1 (15.5-ounce) can coconut milk, full-fat and unsweetened

½ cup water

56 grams or ½ cup oil-roasted peanuts

15 grams or ¼ cup chopped cilantro, stems and leaves

Salt to taste

Optional: red pepper flakes

1. Heat the coconut oil and palm oil in a sauté pan over medium heat. Add the onion and curry powder and sauté until the onions are soft. Add the sliced chicken and sauté until the chicken is opaque. Add the garlic and ginger and stir very well to combine.

2. Pour the coconut milk and water over the chicken. Add the peanuts and stir to combine. Bring the coconut milk to a simmer and cook for about 15 minutes, the curry should be slightly thickened and the chicken cooked thoroughly. Turn off the heat and stir in the chopped cilantro and taste for seasoning. Add red pepper flakes to taste, if desired. Divide into six portions and serve over 100 grams or 1 cup of cooked Cauliflower Rice (page 92).

Baked Cod with Roased Red Pepper Sauce, page 77

Basic Quiche, page 16

Beef and Mushroom Stew, page 58

Breakfast Porridge, page 13

Breakfast Taco, page 18

Buffalo Chicken Meatballs, page 63

Butternut Squash Soup, page 38

Caesar Salad, page 26

Cheese Steak Plate, page 56

Chicken Peanut Curry, page 61

Chicken Piccata, page 65

Cinnamon Chayote Squash, page 128

Chicken Salad, page 32

Creamed Spinach, page 98

Ham and Cheese Puffs, page 48

German Red Cabbage, page 94

Mediterranean Tuna Salad, page 30

Miso Beef, page 57

Coconut Lime Popsicles, page 126

Classic Beef Chili, page 54

Creamy Balsamic Chicken, page 64

Pork Carnitas with Chimichurri Sauce, page 72

Pork Tenderloin with Dijon Sauce and Rutabaga Noodles, page 70

Vegan Taco Salad, page 75

Hempseed Tabouli, page 86

Tomato and Baby Mozzarella Salad, page 87

Yogurt Base with Orange Concentrate, pages 6 and 9

Moussaka, page 68

Simple Roasted Cauliflower, page 91

Smoked Salmon Dip, page 44

Roasted Eggplant Dip, page 42

Spinach and Grilled Radicchio Salad with Bacon Vinaigrette, page 28

Buffalo Chicken Meatballs

NUTRITION FACTS   Makes 4 Servings

Each Serving Provides:

1:27 Ratio

Calories: 407

Carbohydrate: 1.41 grams

Protein: 25.03 grams

Fat: 33.52 grams

When buying pepper sauces, look for ones that contain mostly vinegar, peppers, water, and spices. Avoid any brands that use sweeteners or carbohydrate-based thickening agents such as cornstarch. Buffalo sauce is typically pepper sauce mixed with a lot of butter, this works fantastic for ketogenic recipes. This dish packs a punch. Try the buffalo sauce on anything that needs a flavor boost. Cauliflower is especially good!

454 grams or 1 pound ground chicken breast, or diced whole chicken breast

56 grams or ½ stick butter

125 grams or 1¼ cup sliced celery

60 grams or ½ cup Frank's RedHot Buffalo Wings Sauce

54 grams or ¼ cup light olive oil

115 grams or ½ cup full-fat sour cream, divided into 4 servings (⅛-cup each)

Salt and pepper to taste

Optional: garlic powder to taste

1. Season the ground chicken breast with salt, pepper, and garlic powder if desired. Form the ground chicken into golf ball-size meatballs.

2. In a nonstick skillet, melt the butter over medium to high heat. Brown the meatballs in the melted butter, turning several times to brown each side.

3. Once the meatballs are browned, reduce the heat to low. Add the celery, hot sauce, and olive oil. Stir very well to combine the sauce ingredients.

4. Simmer the meatballs in the sauce until the meatballs are completely cooked through and the celery has softened about 15 to 20 minutes.

5. Divide the meatballs and sauce into four equal servings and top with the sour cream. Serve alongside a simple iceberg salad with blue cheese dressing to complete the meal.

Creamy Balsamic Chicken

NUTRITION FACTS (with green beans) Makes 4 Servings

Each Serving Provides:

1:32 Ratio

Calories: 521

Carbohydrate: 6.16 grams

Protein: 26.62 grams

Fat: 43.28 grams

NUTRITION FACTS (without green beans) Makes 4 Servings

Each Serving Provides:

1:44 Ratio

Calories: 492

Carbohydrate: 3.38 grams

Protein: 25.61 grams

Fat: 41.80 grams

Balsamic vinegar and heavy cream make the most delectable sauce. If you have guests for dinner, consider this dish!

454 grams or 1 pound chicken breast

85 grams or ¾ stick butter

240 grams or 1 cup 36% heavy cream

30 grams or 2 tablespoons balsamic vinegar

3 grams or 1 teaspoon minced fresh garlic (about 1 clove)

7 grams or ⅛ cup chopped fresh parsley

Salt and pepper to taste

1. Cut the chicken breast into bite size pieces. Season with salt and pepper.

2. Melt the butter in a nonstick skillet over medium heat. Add the chicken to the melted butter and brown on all sides.

3. Add the cream, vinegar, and garlic to the chicken. Bring the cream sauce to a slow simmer. Simmer the chicken in the cream sauce until the chicken is cooked through and the cream sauce has thickened, about 15 to 20 minutes. Finish the sauce by stirring in the chopped parsley.

4. Divide the chicken and sauce into four equal servings and serve with 44 grams or ⅓ cup steamed fresh green beans.

Chicken Piccata

NUTRITION FACTS Makes 4 Servings

Each Serving Provides:

1.68:1 Ratio

Calories: 542

Carbohydrate: 2.32 grams

Protein: 26.03 grams

Fat: 47.67 grams

You will never even know this is a low-carb dish. Using prepared tortillas as bread crumbs gives the "fried" crunch to the chicken. Lemon and capers make a bright, flavorful sauce. Try substituting the Swanson Chicken Broth with my Homemade Chicken Broth (page 35) and adjust the nutritional information accordingly.

Make a double or triple batch and freeze the entire meal in 9 × 9-inch foil pans. This is a great meal to pull from the freezer and reheat on a busy night. This will take about 30 to 40 minutes to reheat in a 350°F oven. It is also fantastic when served with celery root puree.

454 grams or 1 pound chicken breast (about two large breasts)

36 grams or ⅓ cup Quick and Easy Low-Carb Bread Crumbs (page 46)

1.5 grams or ½ teaspoon garlic powder

½ teaspoon salt

85 grams or ¾ of a stick of butter

108 grams or ½ cup extra virgin olive oil

117 grams or ½ cup Swanson Chicken Broth, 100% Natural

61 grams or ¼ cup lemon juice

45 grams or ¼ cup capers

0.5 grams or ⅛ teaspoon xanthan gum

Optional: a few sprigs of fresh parsley

Optional: pepper to taste

1. Cut each chicken breast in half so you have four pieces of equal size. Lay each piece between two sheets of wax paper. Using a rolling pin, flatten each piece until it is even in thickness and about ½-inch thick.

2. On a clean sheet of wax paper, combine the bread crumbs, garlic powder, and salt. Coat each piece of chicken with the bread crumbs. There should be enough bread crumbs for an even, thin coating on all sides of the chicken. Do not discard any remaining bread crumbs.

3. Melt the butter in a large skillet over medium heat. Once the butter has melted, add the olive oil. When the butter and olive oil are hot, add the breaded chicken pieces. Fry them on each side for about two to three minutes or until the bread crumb coating is golden brown and crisp. Once each side is cooked, remove the chicken from the pan to a plate and set aside. Do not drain any fat from the pan.

4. Lower the heat from low to medium. Add the chicken broth, lemon juice, capers, any remaining bread crumbs, and xanthan gum to the pan and whisk very well to combine all ingredients. Return the chicken and drippings to the pan and allow the sauce and chicken to simmer until the chicken is completely cooked through and the sauce has thickened, about 10 minutes. There should be approximately 1 cup of sauce remaining.

5. Garnish the chicken with fresh parsley and ground pepper if desired. Serve each piece of chicken with about ¼ cup of the sauce and enjoy.

Chicken Enchiladas

NUTRITION FACTS   **Makes 4 Servings**

Each Serving Provides:

1.18:1 Ratio

Calories: 511

Carbohydrate: 5.87 grams

Protein: 29.13 grams

Fat: 41.23 grams

Chicken enchiladas are usually a crowd pleaser. This recipe is made even easier to assemble since the ingredients are not rolled in the tortillas. This allows less tortilla and carbohydrate to be used while still providing traditional flavors.

280 grams or 2 cups shredded cooked chicken breast

115 grams or ½ cup full-fat sour cream

108 grams or ½ cup extra virgin olive oil

72 grams or 2 La Tortilla Factory Low Carb, High Fiber Tortillas cut into thin strips

1 cup of Tomatillo Salsa (page 115)

57 grams or ½ cup shredded Monterey Jack cheese

Salt and pepper to taste

Optional: pinch of ground cumin

1. Preheat the oven to 350°F. Lightly grease a 9- × 9-inch glass baking dish.

2. In a mixing bowl, add the shredded chicken, sour cream, olive oil, and tortilla strips. Stir very well to evenly combine all ingredients. Season with salt, pepper, and a pinch of cumin if desired. Transfer the mixture to the baking dish and spread into an even layer.

3. Spread the Tomatillo Salsa evenly over the chicken mixture. Finish by sprinkling the shredded cheese over the salsa.

4. Bake for 30 to 40 minutes or until the edges have slightly browned and are bubbling. The cheese should be completely melted and golden brown. Cover with foil if the top begins to brown too quickly. Allow to cool for 30 minutes before serving.

Moussaka

NUTRITION FACTS **Makes 6 Servings**

Each Serving Provides:

1.7:1 Ratio

588 calories

Carbohydrate: 4.89 grams

Protein: 22.92 grams

Fat: 47.29 grams

Moussaka is a Middle Eastern dish with many variations. Some versions use potato, but for ketogenic diets, eggplant is a better choice since it is low in carbohydrate. The topping has been reworked using a combination of two cheeses and cream. Together, the flavors in this dish create a rich and satisfying meal.

454 grams or 1 pound eggplant (buy a little extra)

108 grams or ½ cup extra virgin olive oil

40 grams or ¼ cup diced yellow onion

454 grams or 1 pound ground New Zealand lamb

3 grams or 1 teaspoon minced garlic

1 gram or 1 teaspoon dried oregano

1.5 grams or ½ teaspoon cinnamon

Pinch of dried all spice

125 grams or ½ cup tomato puree

56 grams or ½ stick butter

120 grams or ½ cup 36% heavy cream

50 grams or ½ cup grated Parmesan cheese

28 grams or 2 tablespoons crème fraiche

Salt to taste

1. Preheat the oven to 350°F. Prepare a 2½-quart casserole dish by coating the inside lightly with olive oil.

2. Wash and dry the eggplant. Slice off the stem end. Dice the eggplant into 1-inch cubes.

3. Heat the olive oil in a nonstick skillet over medium heat until it shimmers. Add the diced eggplant and onion. Sauté until the moisture from the eggplant has cooked off and all of the oil has absorbed. The eggplant should be very tender. Transfer to the prepared casserole and spread into an even layer.

4. To the same skillet, add the ground lamb, garlic, oregano, cinnamon, and all spices. Use a potato masher or fork to break the lamb into small pieces. Continue to cook the lamb until it is no longer pink and completely cooked though. Add the tomato puree and stir very well to combine. Season the mixture with salt if needed. Once completely cooked, transfer the lamb mixture to the casserole dish making sure to scrape the skillet very well. Spread the lamb over the eggplant in one even layer.

5. Melt the butter in a small pot over low heat. Once the butter is melted, add the heavy cream, Parmesan cheese, and crème fraiche. Use a whisk to continuously stir the cheese mixture. Cook until the Parmesan is completely melted. Pour the cheese mixture over the lamb in the casserole dish making sure to evenly distribute the cheese.

6. Cover the dish with foil. Pierce the center of the foil to allow steam to escape.

7. Bake for 30 to 40 minutes. Remove the casserole from the oven and allow it to rest for at least 30 minutes. This will help the fat reabsorb. Slice into six equal portions and serve.

Pork Tenderloin with Dijon Sauce and Rutabaga Noodles

NUTRITION FACTS (with rutabaga) Makes 6 Servings

Each Serving Provides:

1:17 Ratio

Calories: 318

Carbohydrate: 4.25 grams

Protein: 26.45 grams

Fat: 25.63 grams

NUTRITION FACTS (without rutabaga) Makes 6 Servings

Each Serving Provides:

1:17 Ratio

Calories: 304

Carbohydrate: 1.39 grams

Protein: 17.11 grams

Fat: 25.53 grams

Rutabaga looks like a turnip but it is yellow on the bottom with a purple top. They are usually quite large and coated in wax. Buy more than you think you need. You will lose quite a bit of vegetable as you peal it. Boiling the rutabaga helps to decrease the bitter flavor as does the Dijon mustard.

340 grams or ¾ pound fresh rutabaga (buy at least 1½ pounds)

454 grams or 1 pound whole pork tenderloin

56 grams or ½ stick butter

54 grams or ¼ cup extra virgin olive oil

240 grams or 1 cup chicken broth, Swanson Chicken Broth, 100% natural

120 grams or ½ cup 36% heavy cream

30 grams or 2 tablespoons Dijon mustard

0.5 grams or ½ teaspoon dried thyme

Salt and pepper to taste

1. Bring a pot of salt water to a boil. Slice off both ends of the rutabaga. Use a sharp knife to slice off the tough outer peal. Use a spiral slicer to shred it into noodle shapes. Boil the rutabaga noodles in the water for about five to seven minutes or until they are soft and tender but not mushy. Drain and set aside. If you do not have a spiralizer, boil and mash the rutabaga adding a little water if necessary.

2. Slice the pork tenderloin into 12 slices. Heat the butter and olive oil in a nonstick skillet over medium heat. Sauté the pork slices in the butter and olive oil until they are slightly browned, flipping once to cook each side. Transfer the cooked pork slices to a plate and set aside. Do not drain any fat from the pan.

3. To the butter and olive oil, add the chicken broth, heavy cream, Dijon mustard, and dried thyme. Use a whisk to combine all the ingredients. Season with salt and pepper if needed. Return the pork slices and all drippings to the sauce. Simmer on low to medium heat until the pork is cooked thoroughly and the sauce has thickened, about 10 to 15 minutes.

4. To serve, place about ½ cup or a quarter of the total amount of the rutabaga noodles on a plate. Top the noodles with two slices of pork tenderloin and about ½ cup of the sauce. Enjoy with a side salad.

Pork Carnitas with Chimichurri Sauce

NUTRITION FACTS (with chimichurri) Makes 16 Servings

Recipe Yields: 8 cups	Calories: 364
Serving Size ½ cup	Carbohydrate: 1.63 grams
Each Serving Provides:	Protein: 21.02 grams
1.34:1 Ratio	Fat: 30.39 grams

NUTRITION FACTS (without chimichurri) Makes 16 Servings

Recipe Yields: 8 cups	Calories: 239
Serving Size ½ cup	Carbohydrate: 1.14 grams
Each Serving Provides:	Protein: 20.81 grams
0.77:1 Ratio	Fat: 16.84 grams

Reserve this recipe for a day when you are home and not in a hurry. Even though there is a long cooking time for carnitas, it will be worth the wait and effort! The meat should be falling apart by the time it is done and the juices and fat will have reduced so much they create caramelized crunchy bits worth fighting over. You're in luck though. The recipe will yield about 8 cups of meat from a 4-pound pork shoulder, so there is plenty to share with a crowd or freeze for later.

4 pounds pork shoulder (Boston Butt)

120 grams or ½ cup orange juice, unsweetened

40 grams or ¼ cup diced yellow onion

6 grams or 2 cloves garlic, sliced

2.5 grams or 1 teaspoon cumin seeds

2 bay leaves

1 batch Chimichurri sauce (page 104)

Salt to taste

1. Place the pork shoulder in a large Dutch oven or the heaviest pot you have. Fill the pot with 4 to 6 cups of water covering about three-quarters of the pork. Add the orange juice, onion, garlic, cumin, and bay leaves. Season the water with salt. Cover the pot with a lid and bring the water to a high simmer over medium heat.

2. Simmer the meat with the lid ajar for three to four hours, occasionally flipping the meat to evenly cook both sides. The meat is done when it is very tender and falling apart easily. Do not reduce the liquid to less than 2 cups, add water if needed. The pork can also braise in the oven at 350°F. The cooking time will be the same.

3. Remove the meat from the pot onto a rimmed baking sheet. Do not discard the cooking liquid! As the meat cools, bring the cooking liquid to a high simmer to reduce the lliquid until there are two cups remaining.

4. While the cooking liquid is reducing, shred the meat, discarding any skin, bones, and tough gristle. Keep all pieces of fat and return them to the pot of cooking liquid as you are shredding the meat. Remove the bay leaves.

5. Once all of the meat is shredded, return it to the pot of reduced cooking liquid and stir very well to coat. At this point, you can freeze the meat in freezer-safe zip-top bags for future meals.

6. Just prior to serving, put the pot over high heat and let the bottom layer of meat begin to crisp and caramelize in the reduced cooking liquid and fat. Once you see brown crispy bits of meat near the edges, turn the heat off, and stir the meat for the last time. Serve the meat with two tablespoons Chimichurri sauce.

Stuffed Poblano Peppers

NUTRITION FACTS   **Makes 6 Servings**

Serving Size: ½ pepper

Each Serving Provides:

1:22 Ratio

Calories: 402 calories

Carbohydrate: 5.16 grams

Protein: 21.69 grams

Fat: 32.78 grams

Try to find large poblano peppers. If the peppers you find are too small and you are not able to fit the filling into six equal portions, don't worry! Simply slice the peppers into thin strips and lay them in an even layer on top of the salsa on the bottom of the baking dish. Assemble the ingredients in the same order and bake for the same amount of time.

454 grams or 1 pound ground pork

108 grams or ½ cup extra virgin olive oil

1 gram or 1 teaspoon chili powder

125 grams or 1 cup plus ¼ cup shredded cheddar cheese (divided)

300 grams or 3 large poblano peppers, deseeded and cut in half lengthwise

1 batch or 1 cup of Low-Carbohydrate Salsa (page 114)

Optional: 1 tablespoon ground flaxseed meal

1. Preheat the oven to 425°F.

2. Heat skillet over medium to high heat. Add the ground pork, olive oil, and chili powder and sauté until completely cooked through. Use a potato masher to help break the meat into small pieces. Once the pork is completely cooked, turn off the heat and add 1 cup of the shredded cheese. Stir until the cheese is completely melted. Set this mixture aside to cool slightly.

3. Pour the salsa into a 2½-quart baking dish. Place the pepper halves on top of the salsa cut sides up.

4. Fill each pepper half with one sixth of the meat filling. Use the remaining ¼ cup of shredded cheese to sprinkle on top of all the filled peppers. Bake uncovered for 30 to 40 minutes. Some oil will cook out; do your best to redistribute it evenly over the peppers. You could also add 1 tablespoon of ground flaxseed meal to the pork mixture to help it retain the oil.

5. Serve with avocado slices or sour cream for extra fat.

Vegan Taco Salad

NUTRITION FACTS (with salsa) Makes 4 Servings

Each Serving Provides:

1:93 Ratio

Calories: 334

Carbohydrate: 3.95 grams

Protein: 11.68 grams

Fat: 30.10 grams

NUTRITION FACTS (with 2 tablespoons of salsa) Makes 4 Servings

Each Serving Provides:

1:63 Ratio

Calories: 349

Carbohydrate: 6.56 grams

Protein: 12.12 grams

Fat: 30.45 grams

This is not your typical taco salad. The "meat" mixture is a combination of nuts and hempseeds, a great option for a meat-free meal!

60 grams ½ cup whole almonds

60 grams or ½ cup whole macadamia nuts

4 grams or ½ tablespoon chili powder

68 grams or ½ cup hempseeds

228 grams or 4 cups chopped iceberg lettuce

68 grams or ½ of an avocado, sliced into 8 slices

Salt and pepper to taste

1 batch or 1 cup Low-Carbohydrate Salsa (page 114)

1. In a large bowl, combine the almonds and macadamia nuts. Cover the nuts with water and soak for two hours. This will soften the nuts. After two hours, drain and rinse the nuts. Combine the chili powder and nuts in a food processor. Grind them into a coarse nut meal. They may be as crunchy or as smooth as you like. Once the nuts are ground, mix the hempseeds with the nut mixture. Stir well and set aside.

2. Assemble the taco salad by placing ½ cup of the nut mixture on top of 1 cup of chopped iceberg lettuce. Top with two slices of avocado and 2 tablespoons of salsa. You can also create a lettuce bowl by slicing a whole lettuce head in half and removing the center leaves until you have a 57-gram portion.

Egg and Cauliflower Fried Rice

NUTRITION FACTS   **Makes 6 Servings**

Recipe Yields: 8 cups

Serving Size: 1⅓ cup

Each Serving Provides:

1:99 Ratio

Calories: 428

Carbohydrate: 4.39 grams

Protein: 15.11 grams

Fat: 38.87 grams

A low-carbohydrate version of a favorite take out dish! This is a great use of Cauliflower Rice, the strong flavors from the sesame oil and soy sauce help hide the flavor of the cauliflower.

600 grams or 12 medium eggs or 10 large eggs

108 grams or ½ cup canola oil

54 grams or ¼ cup coconut oil, divided

15 grams or 1 tablespoon toasted sesame oil

400 grams or 4 cups raw Cauliflower Rice (page 92)

140 grams or 2 cups shredded cabbage

64 grams or ¼ cup soy sauce

12 grams or 2 tablespoons sliced green onions

Optional: salt and pepper to taste

Optional: red chili flakes to taste

1. Break the eggs into a bowl and then add the canola oil. Use a fork to break the yolks and combine the eggs with the oil.

2. Heat a nonstick skillet over low to medium heat. Add 1 tablespoon of the coconut oil. Pour the egg and oil mixture into the pan. Scramble the eggs just until they are set. Remove the eggs from the pan and set aside.

3. In the same pan, add the remaining coconut oil, sesame oil, riced cauliflower, and shredded cabbage. Increase the heat to medium. Sauté the vegetables until the cabbage and cauliflower are tender, about five minutes.

4. Return the scrambled eggs and any liquid to the pan with the cauliflower. Add the soy sauce and sliced green onions to the mixture. Stir very well to combine. Heat the mixture for an additional one to two minutes or until all vegetables are cooked thoroughly and the eggs are hot. Season with salt, pepper, and red chili flakes if desired, divide into six portions of approximately 1⅓ cups each, and enjoy.

Baked Cod with Roasted Red Pepper Sauce

NUTRITION FACTS   **Makes 6 Servings**

Each Serving Provides:

1.48:1 Ratio

Calories: 451

Carbohydrate: 7.17 grams

Protein: 18.91 grams

Fat: 38.54 grams

No boring white fish when paired with red pepper sauce! This is not a spicy dish, but rich with butter and smoky red pepper flavor. Zucchini noodles add a satisfying touch, but if you are in a hurry use fresh spinach or other greens.

510 grams or six 3-ounce cod filets, skinned and deboned

908 grams or 2½ pounds zucchini (about 10 small zucchini)

¼ cup water

2 batches or 3 cups Roasted Red Pepper Sauce (page 102)

Salt and pepper to taste

1. Preheat the oven to 400°F. Lightly grease a 9- x 9-inch glass baking dish.

2. Arrange the cod filets in the dish so they are not touching. Season the filets with salt and pepper. Cover the dish with foil and bake for about 15 to 20 minutes or until the filets are completely opaque and flake easily.

3. Prepare the zucchini by first washing them under cold water and then slicing off the stem end. Use a spiral slicer to cut the zucchini into "noodles." If you do not have a spiral slicer, slice them into small matchsticks. You should have 2 pounds of prepared zucchini.

4. Place the sliced zucchini in a glass bowl and add ¼ cup water. Cover the bowl with a plate and steam in a microwave for two to three minutes or until the zucchini are bright green and slightly softened. Drain excess water.

5. Serve the cod filets with ½ cup of Roasted Red Pepper Sauce.

Coconut Shrimp with Peanut Sauce

Use frozen prepared shrimp, and this recipe comes together very fast! Completely thaw the shrimp, rinse under cold water, and dry very well on paper towels prior to coating.

15 grams or 1 tablespoon egg white (about half of a large egg)

15 grams or 1 tablespoon extra virgin olive oil

454 grams or 1 pound large shrimp, peeled and deveined with the tail still attached

30 grams or 6 tablespoons finely shredded coconut, unsweetened

1 batch or ½ cup Peanut Sauce (page 119)

1. Preheat the oven to 450°F. Line a baking sheet with parchment paper.

2. In a large mixing bowl, combine the egg white and olive oil, whisk with a fork until combined. Add the shrimp to the egg white mixture and toss to evenly coat.

3. Once the shrimp is coated with the egg mixture, sprinkle the coconut over the top. Use a spatula to toss the shrimp with the coconut until they are evenly coated. Lay the shrimp in a single layer on the parchment-covered baking sheet.

4. Bake the shrimp for about 5 to 10 minutes. Be careful to not overcook! The shrimp are ready when they are bright orange on the outside and opaque white in the center. The coconut will brown on the edges and create a crisp coating. You can also help the coconut brown and crisp by turning on the broiler and setting the pan on the very top rack, but do not take your eyes off of them! Divide the shrimp into four portions and serve with ⅛ cup of the Peanut Sauce.

Deviled Clams

NUTRITION FACTS **Makes 2 Servings**

Serving Size: 2 ramekins or 4 clamshells

Each Serving Provides:

1.3:1 Ratio

Calories: 468

Carbohydrate: 5.97 grams

Protein: 23.84 grams

Fat: 38.70 grams

Canned clams are readily available and are great to use in this recipe. If you have fresh clams, steam them first, being sure to remove any gritty parts before combining with the remaining ingredients. Using the Fiber Rolls (page 4) in this recipe produces an almost muffin-like result. The outside is crispy and the center should remain very soft and most. Serve with Classic Tartar Sauce (page 117) for extra fat if needed. You can easily make a fun appetizer from this recipe by filling cleaned mini clam shells (steamers) instead of ramekins or larger clamshells.

½ batch of baked Fiber Rolls, cut into large cubes

140 grams or 1 cup drained, minced steamed clams [about 2 (6.5-ounce) cans]

56 grams or ½ stick butter

15 grams or ¼ cup chopped fresh parsley

0.5 grams or ⅛ teaspoon onion powder

0.5 grams or ⅛ teaspoon garlic powder

Salt and pepper to taste

Optional: paprika to taste

1. Preheat the oven to 425°F. Place 4 ramekins or 8 clamshells on a foil-lined baking sheet.

2. Place the cubes of Fiber Rolls into a food processor. Pulse the blade until the rolls are chopped into very fine bread crumbs.

3. Add the remaining ingredients to the food processor and continue to pulse until completely combined.

4. Divide the mixture into equal portions and fill the ramekins or clam shells. Sprinkle the tops with paprika if using. Bake for 15 to 20 minutes or until the clam mixture has puffed up and turned golden brown.

Sriracha Scallop Roll

NUTRITION FACTS   Makes 4 servings

Recipe Yields: 4 roll ups

Serving Size: 1 roll up

Each Serving Provides:

0.72:1 Ratio

Calories: 257

Carbohydrate: 3.75 grams

Protein: 20.67 grams

Fat: 17.63 grams

A cross between sushi and a burrito! All the great sushi flavors are here without all of the carbs. This dish should be served with a high-fat side such as Cucumber and Avocado Relish (page 88) or Peanut Spaghetti Squash (page 100). Try adding pea shoots inside the roll for extra flavor and crunch.

454 grams or 1 pound raw sea scallops, cleaned

59 grams or ¼ cup mayonnaise

7 grams or ½ tablespoon sriracha sauce

16 grams or 8 large sheets SeaSnax seaweed snacks

136 grams or 1 avocado

1. Dry the scallops very well on paper towels. Lightly grease a nonstick pan with oil and heat over medium heat. Sear the scallops on both sides until completely cooked through. The flesh will opaque through the entire scallop. Do not overcrowd the pan. The scallops will release a lot of liquid while they are cooking. If allowed to cook in the liquid they will become soggy.

2. If the scallops are large, chop them into bite size pieces. Mix the cooked scallops with the mayonnaise and Sriracha sauce.

3. Lay two sheets of the seaweed on a cutting board. Offset them slightly to make a wider rolling surface. Place one-quarter of the scallop mixture on top of the seaweed. Add a quarter of the avocado slices and any additional fillings. Roll the scallops and seaweed, folding in the edges—similar to a burrito. Place the roll seam side down on a plate and serve immediately.

VEGETABLES AND SIDE DISHES

Coleslaw

German Turnip Salad

Hempseed Tabouli

Tomato and Baby Mozzarella Salad

Cucumber and Avocado Relish

Kale Shreds

Roasted Cabbage Noodles

Roasted Broccoli with Almonds

Cauliflower Rice

Simple Roasted Cauliflower

German Red Cabbage

Sautéed Savory Mushrooms

Turnip and Cauliflower Mash

Grilled Balsamic Radicchio

Creamed Spinach

Zucchini and Onion Gratin

Peanut Spaghetti Squash

Coleslaw

NUTRITION FACTS **Makes 12 Servings**

Recipe Yields: 6 cups

Serving Size: ½ cup

Each Serving Provides:

3.13:1 Ratio

Calories: 121

Carbohydrate: 2.77 grams

Protein: 1.00 grams

Fat: 11.81 grams

This is a "no-frills" coleslaw recipe. It is delicious on its own and can easily accommodate other additions such as shredded carrot, bell peppers, and herbs to make it more interesting. When made as follows, it is reminiscent of deli-style coleslaw that is slightly sweet and tangy.

907 grams or 2 pounds green cabbage (buy a cabbage that is at least 2½ pounds)

20 grams or ⅛ cup finely minced yellow onion

176 grams or ¾ cup mayonnaise

30 grams or 2 tablespoons cider vinegar

7 grams or 1½ teaspoons Truvia (2 packets)

Salt and pepper to taste

1. Remove any dark green leaves from the cabbage. Rinse if necessary. Cut the cabbage into quarters and remove the tough core. Use a food processor slicing blade to shred the cabbage very quickly, or slice the quartered portions very finely with a sharp knife.

2. In a large bowl, toss the cabbage with the remaining ingredients until it is completely coated. Season with salt and pepper; be careful to not over salt.

3. Cover the bowl and refrigerate for at least two hours. The cabbage will soften and wilt significantly. Serve alongside Pork Carnitas with Chimichurri Sauce (page 72).

German Turnip Salad

NUTRITION FACTS   Makes 8 Servings

Recipe Yields: 4 cups

Serving Size: ½ cup

Each Serving Provides:

1.15:1 Ratio

Calories: 167

Carbohydrate: 3.77 grams

Protein: 7.86 grams

Fat: 13.39 grams

How do you make turnips taste better? Pair them with bacon! The egg yolks in the recipe play an important role, too. Turnips do not have the same starchy quality as potatoes. Instead they have a waxy and smooth texture. When the hard-boiled egg yolks are added, the texture from the yolks mimics the starch of potatoes, further helping to create a delicious, low-carb potato salad replacement. Weigh the turnips as instructed. To further improve the flavor, cut them into smaller pieces before boiling.

500 grams or 4 cups diced turnips, about ½ inch pieces (buy at least 1½ pounds)

120 grams or 4 sliced raw bacon

45 grams or 3 tablespoons canola oil

30 grams or 2 tablespoons red wine vinegar

68 grams or 4 hard-boiled egg yolks, crumbled

12 grams or 2 tablespoons sliced scallions

3.5 grams or ¾ teaspoon Truvia (1 packet)

Salt and pepper to taste

1. Place the diced turnips into a pot and cover with water. Bring to a boil and cook until tender. Drain and rinse the turnips. Set aside.

2. Dice the bacon strips into small pieces. Heat a pot over medium heat and fry the bacon pieces until crisp. Do not drain any of the fat. Add the cooked turnips to the pot with the bacon. Stir very well to evenly coat the turnips with the bacon and bacon fat.

3. Add all remaining ingredients to the turnips and bacon. Stir very well to combine. Serve the salad warm or room temperature. Refrigerate for storage.

Hempseed Tabouli

NUTRITION FACTS   **Makes 6 Servings**

Recipe Yields: 3 cups	Calories: 249
Serving Size: ½ cup	Carbohydrate: 2.28 grams
Each Serving Provides:	Protein: 8.95 grams
2:1 Ratio	Fat: 22.68 grams

Tabouli is a traditional Mediterranean salad made with fresh parsley. Be sure to clean the parsley thoroughly before chopping. Remove the tough stems from the bottom of the parsley, leaving only the leafy green tops. Submerge the parsley tops in a large bowl of cold water and wash them very well. Change the water once. Allow any sand to sink to the bottom of the bowl, then remove and dry the parsley and chop. Instead of bulgur this recipe uses hempseeds, which are lower in carbohydrates and higher in fat and protein.

120 grams or 2 cups finely chopped fresh flat leaf parsley (about 1 bunch)

135 grams or 1 cup hempseeds

72 grams or ⅓ cup extra virgin olive oil

61 grams or ¼ cup freshly squeezed lemon juice

34 grams or ¼ cup diced tomato

12 grams or 2 tablespoons sliced green onion

Salt and pepper to taste

1. Combine the parsley with all remaining ingredients and stir very well to combine. Season with salt and pepper. This is best served the next day when all the flavors have had time to combine and the parsley has softened.

Tomato and Baby Mozzarella Salad

NUTRITION FACTS   **Makes 6 Servings**

Serving Size: ½ cup

Each Serving Provides:

1.03:1 Ratio

Calories: 69

Carbohydrate: 1.56 grams

Protein: 3.65 grams

Fat: 5.39 grams

Sometimes, no extra fat is needed to make a ketogenic recipe. A simple combination of three ingredients makes a fantastic side dish. You can also make this into an easy appetizer by skewering one of each ingredient onto a toothpick. Fresh basil leaves, when in season, make an excellent addition. Try to find tomatoes and mozzarella that are approximately the same. If that is not possible, slice the ingredients into similar sizes.

112 grams or 1 cup cherry tomatoes

112 grams or 1 cup drained ciliegine (cherry-size fresh mozzarella)

112 grams or 1 cup pitted kalamata olives

1. Combine all ingredients in a bowl and stir gently to combine and serve.

Cucumber and Avocado Relish

NUTRITION FACTS   **Makes 10 Servings**

Recipe Yields: 2½ cups

Serving Size: ¼ cup

Each Serving Provides:

2.13:1 Ratio

Calories: 47

Carbohydrate: 1.58 grams

Protein: 0.43 grams

Fat: 4.28 grams

260 grams or 2 cups finely diced English cucumber (about 1–1½ English cucumbers)

100 or 1 cup finely diced avocado

40 grams or ¼ cup finely diced onion

30 grams or 2 tablespoons freshly squeezed lime juice

27 grams or ⅛ cup extra virgin olive oil

0.5 grams or ⅛ teaspoon garlic powder

Salt and pepper to taste

Optional: red pepper flakes to taste

1. Place all ingredients in a bowl and toss gently to combine. Season with salt, pepper, and red pepper flakes if desired. Allow this to sit for two hours before serving. The salt and lime juice will soften the onion and cucumber and draw out some of the natural liquid. Cover and refrigerate.

2. Gently toss again just before serving.

Kale Shreds

NUTRITION FACTS (Lacinato) Makes 8 Servings

Recipe Yields: 4 cups	Calories: 15
Serving Size: ½ cup	Carbohydrate: 2.07 grams
Each Serving Provides:	Protein: 1.08 grams
0.07:1 Ratio	Fat: 0.23 grams

NUTRITION FACTS (Scotch) Makes 8 Servings

Recipe Yields: 4 cups	Calories: 25
Serving Size: ½ cup	Carbohydrate: 3.76 grams
Each Serving Provides:	Protein: 1.59 grams
0.06:1 Ratio	Fat: 0.34 grams

Kale can be difficult to eat in its raw state, but when treated properly, it is a great base vegetable for salads. Curly (Scotch) or flat (Lacinato) kale can both be prepared with this method. Buy at least 1½ pounds of kale to yield 4 cups or 1 pound of prepared, stemless leaves.

1 bunch of kale leaves, choose bright green, firm, and undamaged leaves

¼ teaspoon salt

1 teaspoon cider vinegar

1. Remove the tender leaves from the tough stem by holding the stem in one hand and quickly pulling the leaf off by pinching your fingers against the stem, working from stem to tip with one pass. You should be left holding the thickest portion of the stem.

2. Submerge the leaves in a bowl of cold water, swishing them several times. Let the leaves and water sit for several minutes to allow any dirt and sand to settle on the bottom. Remove the leaves from the water and dry them very well by rolling them in paper towels.

3. Cut the washed leaves into thin strands. Return the leaves to a large bowl and sprinkle the salt and vinegar over them. Use your hands to squeeze and toss the leaves. You want to squeeze hard enough to begin breaking down the tough leaves. The salt and vinegar will continue to soften the leaves.

4. Refrigerate the leaves in a large zip-top bag for about three days.

Roasted Cabbage Noodles

NUTRITION FACTS   **Makes 8 Servings**

Recipe Yields: 4 cups	Calories: 80
Serving Size: ½ cup	Carbohydrate: 3.75 grams
Each Serving Provides:	Protein: 1.45 grams
1.27:1 Ratio	Fat: 6.59 grams

A simple side dish that goes well with everything. Coconut oil adds a touch of natural sweetness to the cabbage but is not overpowering. Slice the cabbage lengthwise into long strips and you will have strands to twirl around your fork.

908 grams or 2 pounds sliced green cabbage (about 1 medium head)

54 grams or ¼ cup melted coconut oil

Pinch of salt

1. Preheat the oven to 425°F. Line two baking sheets with aluminum foil.
2. Divide the sliced cabbage in half onto the two baking sheets. Drizzle the coconut oil onto the cabbage and then sprinkle with salt. Use your hands to toss the cabbage, oil, and salt together until all the cabbage is lightly coated with the oil. Spread the cabbage into one thin, even layer.
3. Bake the cabbage for 15 minutes. After 15 minutes, use a spatula to stir the cabbage, making sure to scrape the pieces on the edge of the baking sheet into the center. Redistribute the cabbage into one even layer and return to the oven for 15 additional minutes.
4. The cabbage is finished when it is tender. There will be some charred pieces and some that are still green. Stir the cabbage again and serve.

Roasted Broccoli with Almonds

NUTRITION FACTS **Makes 8 Servings**

Recipe Yields: 4 cups

Serving Size: ½ cup

Each Serving Provides:

1.78:1 Ratio

Calories: 123

Carbohydrate: 2.89 grams

Protein: 3.26 grams

Fat: 10.92 grams

This is another simple side dish that can be served along with almost anything! The almonds give the broccoli a fantastic crunch that helps make broccoli anything but boring.

454 grams or 1 pound fresh broccoli

54 grams or ¼ cup olive oil

60 grams or ½ cup slivered almonds

Salt and pepper to taste

Optional: garlic powder to taste

1. Preheat the oven to 450°F. Line a baking sheet with parchment paper.
2. Prepare the broccoli by removing any outer green leaves and the thick, woody stem. Rinse under cold water. Cut the broccoli into quarters. Chop each quarter into ½-inch pieces. Do not worry about separating the florets from the stems. Use as much of the stem as possible.
3. Spread the broccoli on the baking sheet. Drizzle the oil and sprinkle salt over the broccoli. Season with pepper and garlic powder, if using. Toss the broccoli with the olive oil and seasonings until it is evenly coated.
4. Arrange the broccoli in a single layer with pieces touching as little as possible on the baking sheet. Roast for 15 minutes.
5. After 15 minutes, remove the pan from the oven. Sprinkle the almonds over the broccoli and use a spatula to toss and flip the broccoli. Arrange in a single layer again and return to the oven for an additional 15 minutes of roasting. Serve immediately.

Cauliflower Rice

Recipe Yields: 4 to 8 cups, depending on the size of the cauliflower

Serving Size: 1 cup

Each Serving Provides:

0.12:1 Ratio

Calories: 19

Carbohydrate: 1.81 grams

Protein: 1.84 grams

Fat: 0.45 grams

It. Goes. With. Everything. Except maybe breakfast. Depending on the size of your cauliflower head, this recipe can yield anywhere from 4 to 8 cups of cauliflower rice.

1 head cauliflower

¼ cup water

Salt and pepper to taste

1. Remove the outer leaves and the bottom of the stem from the cauliflower. Cut the cauliflower into quarters. Chop each quarter into 1-inch pieces.

2. Fill a food processor bowl about half way with the chopped cauliflower. Pulse the cauliflower about 10 to 15 times. The cauliflower should be evenly chopped into "rice" size pieces. Empty the riced cauliflower into a glass bowl and repeat the process with the remaining chopped cauliflower.

3. Put ¼ cup of water in the glass bowl with the riced cauliflower and cover with a lid. Microwave on high for two to five minutes. Remove the bowl from the microwave and stir. Microwave a second time for another two minutes. The cauliflower rice should be tender but not mushy. Season with salt and pepper and serve.

Simple Roasted Cauliflower

NUTRITION FACTS   **Makes 8 Servings**

Recipe Yields: 4 cups

Serving Size: ½ cup

Each Serving Provides:

2.49:1 Ratio

Calories: 73

Carbohydrate: 1.69 grams

Protein: 1.09 grams

Fat: 6.91 grams

Roasted cauliflower is a keto staple! Consider adding dried herbs and spices prior to roasting to enhance the flavor. Although not included in this recipe, dried Italian herbs, herbes de Provence, cumin, curry powder, and chili flakes all add variety. This is a fantastic option to "bulk up" a meal and add lots of needed fiber.

454 grams or 1 pound fresh cauliflower

54 grams or ¼ cup olive oil

Pinch of salt

1. Preheat the oven to 450°F. Line a baking sheet with parchment paper.
2. Remove outer green leaves and stem and rinse the cauliflower under cold water. Cut the cauliflower into quarters. Chop each quarter into ½-inch pieces. Do not worry about separating the florets from the stems.
3. Spread the cauliflower on the baking sheet. Drizzle the oil and the salt over the cauliflower. Toss the cauliflower with the olive oil and salt until it is evenly coated.
4. Arrange the cauliflower on the baking sheet in a single layer, with pieces touching as little as possible. Roast for 15 minutes.
5. After 15 minutes, remove the pan from the oven and use a spatula to toss and flip the cauliflower. Arrange in a single layer again and return to the oven for an additional 15 minutes of roasting. Serve immediately.

German Red Cabbage

NUTRITION FACTS   **Makes 10 Servings**

Recipe Yields: 5 cups

Serving Size: ½ cup

Each Serving Provides:

0.02:1 Ratio

Calories: 26

Carbohydrate: 4.84 grams

Protein: 1.30 grams

Fat: 0.15 grams

Cabbage is a versatile ingredient and perfect for ketogenic recipes. Usually, sugar would be used in this recipe, making it too high in carbohydrates for ketogenic diets. Truvia replaces the sugar but the rest of the ingredients are the same. It tastes just as good! Serve with chicken prepared and cooked in the same way as in the Chicken Piccata recipe (page 65), but omit the piccata sauce and instead top the chicken with butter.

908 grams or 2 pounds red cabbage (buy a slightly heavier cabbage)

25 grams or ¼ cup cider vinegar

7 grams or 1½ teaspoons Truvia (2 packets)

Pinch of salt

2 bay leaves

1. Peal off the outer leaves of the cabbage and rinse the entire head under cold water. Cut it into quarters and remove the tough stem from each quarter. Shred each section in a food processor on the thickest setting. Alternatively, slice the quarters very thinly with a knife to make shreds.

2. Combine all of the ingredients in a large stockpot. Add enough water to reach the top of the cabbage. Simmer at medium heat uncovered for at least two hours—longer is better. The cabbage is ready to eat when it is very tender and most of the water has cooked off. Remove the bay leaves and serve.

Sautéed Savory Mushrooms

NUTRITION FACTS   **Makes 6 Servings**

Recipe Yields: 2 cups

Serving Size: ⅓ cup

Each Serving Provides:

1:1 Ratio

Calories: 53

Carbohydrate: 2.18 grams

Protein: 1.89 grams

Fat: 4.05 grams

Although soy sauce is used in this recipe, these do not take on a strong soy flavor. The soy sauce adds richness and depth to the earthy flavor of the mushrooms, making them the perfect complement to any meal.

454 grams or 1 pound (2 8-ounce packages) baby portabella mushrooms

28 grams or 2 tablespoons of butter

17 grams or 1 tablespoon soy sauce

3.5 grams or ¾ teaspoon Truvia (1 packet)

1. Quickly wash any dirt off the mushrooms. Use as little water as possible to do so. You may also use a pastry brush to brush the dirt off if they are not very dirty. Trim the dry ends from the bottom of the mushrooms and cut them into quarters.
2. Heat the butter in a nonstick skillet over medium high heat until melted. Add the mushrooms, soy sauce, and Truvia to the butter. Sauté the mushrooms until they have released all of their liquid and absorbed the butter. Serve immediately.

Turnip and Cauliflower Mash

NUTRITION FACTS   Makes 8 Servings

Recipe Yields: 4 cups

Serving Size: ½ cup

Each Serving Provides:

1.68:1 Ratio

Calories: 129

Carbohydrate: 4.77 grams

Protein: 1.96 grams

Fat: 11.29 grams

Do not pass over this recipe! The turnip and cauliflower flavors complement each other fantastically. The cauliflower minimizes the turnip flavor, and boiling the two vegetables together helps eliminate any bitterness. The resulting puree is delicious.

Buy small or medium size turnips, larger ones are bitter and become fibrous. Buy more than you need; they will lose quite a bit of weight after peeling them.

454 grams or 1 pound fresh cauliflower (buy a slightly heavier one)

454 grams or 1 pound fresh turnips (about 3–4 medium ones)

120 grams or ½ half cup 36% heavy cream

56 grams or ½ stick butter

Pinch of salt

1. Cut the cauliflower into 1-inch pieces. Use both the stems and florets. Slice the root and stem end off the turnips. Slice off the outer skin with a sharp knife. Cut the pealed turnips into 1-inch cubes.

2. Put the cut cauliflower and turnips into a pot and cover with water. Use as much water as possible. This will help pull out some of the bitterness from the turnips. Salt the water very well. Place the pot over high heat and bring to a boil. Boil the vegetables for about 10 to 15 minutes or until the largest pieces are fork tender. Drain the vegetables into a colander and return to the same pot.

3. Allow the vegetables to "steam off" the excess liquid by sitting in the pot on the hot burner. You are only using the residual heat from the pot and burner. Stir the vegetables a few times.

4. Add the butter and heavy cream to the vegetables. Use an immersion blender to puree.

Grilled Balsamic Radicchio

NUTRITION FACTS   **Makes 6 Servings**

Recipe Yields: 12 wedges

Serving Size: 2 wedges

Each Serving Provides:

0.87:1 Ratio

Calories: 36

Carbohydrate: 2.38 grams

Protein: 0.63 grams

Fat: 2.61 grams

Radicchio is the vegetable that resembles a small red cabbage. It is often passed over because of its bitter taste or simply because people do not know what to do with it. It is best eaten when it has been charred on a grill or under a broiler. Balsamic vinegar and Truvia take away most of the bitterness and transform it into a savory side dish.

258 grams or one 4-inch radicchio (choose one that is bright and firm)

15 grams or 1 tablespoon balsamic vinegar

15 grams or 1 tablespoon extra virgin olive oil

3.5 grams or ¾ teaspoon Truvia (1 packet)

Pinch of salt

1. Preheat a grill or broiler on high heat.
2. Cut the radicchio into 12 thin wedges, leaving the core attached to hold the leaves together.
3. In a large bowl, combine the vinegar, oil, Truvia, and salt. Stir to completely combine. Add the radicchio to the balsamic mixture and toss to evenly coat. Let the radicchio sit in the mixture, tossing several times until the balsamic mixture is absorbed.
4. Grill or broil the radicchio wedges on each side until the edges are slightly charred. This will only take about three to five minutes per side.
5. Store the grilled radicchio in a glass bowl covered tightly.

Creamed Spinach

NUTRITION FACTS   **Makes 4 Servings**

Recipe Yields: 3 cups

Serving Size: ¾ cup

Each Serving Provides:

2.46:1 Ratio

Calories: 197

Carbohydrate: 2.04 grams

Protein: 5.47 grams

Fat: 18.50 grams

Use frozen spinach in this recipe. It has already been washed and cooked, so it is a huge time saver.

284 grams or 1 (10-ounce) box frozen spinach

120 grams or ½ cup 36% heavy cream

25 grams or ¼ cup Parmesan cheese

28 grams or 2 tablespoons butter

Salt and pepper to taste

Optional: pinch of nutmeg

1. Cook the spinach according to package directions. Drain the spinach very well, squeezing out as much water as possible.
2. In a pot, combine the drained spinach and all the remaining ingredients. Stir until the cheese and butter are completely melted. All the ingredients should be evenly combined. Season the spinach with salt and pepper. Add a tiny pinch of freshly grated nutmeg if desired. Serve immediately.

Zucchini and Onion Gratin

NUTRITION FACTS   **Makes 6 Servings**

Each Serving Provides:

1.53:1 Ratio

Calories: 132 Calories

Carbohydrate: 3.33 grams

Protein: 4.11 grams

Fat: 11.42 grams

Zucchini takes on the flavor of other ingredients very well and provides a large serving for very little carbohydrate. In this case, the zucchini, onion, and cheese melt together creating a rich and satisfying gratin.

454 grams or 1 pound small zucchini (about 3–4)

115 grams or ½ cup sliced yellow onion (about 1 medium onion)

50 grams or ½ cup grated Parmesan cheese

54 grams or ¼ cup extra virgin olive oil

Salt and pepper to taste

1. Preheat the oven to 350°F. Lightly grease a 2½-quart casserole dish.
2. Slice the stem end off of the zucchini. Using a mandolin or the slicing blade of a food processor, slice the zucchini into thin rounds.
3. Spread half of the sliced onion in a thin layer on the bottom of the gratin dish. Cover with a thin layer of half of the zucchini rounds. Evenly sprinkle half of the cheese over the zucchini. Season this layer with salt and pepper.
4. Repeat the same process with the second half of the ingredients. After the dish is assembled, drizzle the olive oil over the top of the gratin.
5. Bake for 45 to 50 minutes or until the sides are crisp and the center of the gratin is tender. Allow to rest for 15 minutes before serving. The zucchini will absorb most of the liquid that remains at the bottom. Divide the gratin into six portions and serve.

Peanut Spaghetti Squash

NUTRITION FACTS **Makes 4 Servings**

Each Serving Provides:

2.28:1 Ratio

Calories: 163

Carbohydrate: 4.90 grams

Protein: 1.77 grams

Fat: 15.17grams

310 grams or 2 cups cooked spaghetti squash

54 grams or ¼ cup melted coconut oil (add 1 teaspoon toasted sesame oil for extra flavor)

16 grams or 1 tablespoon natural peanut butter, unsweetened, peanuts only

17 grams or 1 tablespoon soy sauce

12 grams or 2 tablespoons sliced scallions

Salt to taste

Red pepper flakes to taste

1. Preheat the oven to 350°F. Lightly grease a 9 × 9-inch glass baking dish.
2. In a small bowl, combine the coconut oil, peanut butter, soy sauce, scallions, and seasonings. Stir very well to combine.
3. Spread the spaghetti squash into the baking dish. Pour the peanut mixture over the squash. Toss the squash in the peanut mixture to evenly coat.
4. Bake for 30 minutes. Divide into four portions and serve.

DRESSINGS AND SAUCES

Roasted Red Pepper Sauce

Cheese Sauce

Chimichurri Sauce

Guacamole

Tzatziki Sauce

Tahini Dressing

Raspberry Chia Vinaigrette

Dijon Vinaigrette

Bacon Vinaigrette

Veggie Ranch Dressing

Thousand Island Dressing

Chili Powder BBQ Sauce

Low-Carbohydrate Salsa

Tomatillo Salsa

Kale Pesto

Classic Tartar Sauce

Miso Butter

Peanut Sauce

Roasted Red Pepper Sauce

NUTRITION FACTS   **Makes 3 Servings**

Recipe Yields: 1½ cups

Serving Size: ½ cup

Each Serving Provides:

6.27:1 Ratio

Calories: 182

Carbohydrate: 1.99 grams

Protein: 1.01 grams

Fat: 18.82 grams

Looking for a sauce that complements everything? This is it! Try this on simple sautéed fish, grilled chicken and beef, or even Italian sausages. This sauce is one of the most delicious ways to sneak extra fat into your meal.

85 grams or ¾ stick butter

20 grams or ⅛ cup diced yellow onion

250 grams or 1 cup diced roasted red peppers (rinse seeds off)

2.5 grams or 1 teaspoon paprika (sweet or hot depending on what you like)

120 grams or ½ cup 36% heavy cream

Pinch of salt

2 bay leaves

1. In a 2-quart pot over medium heat, sauté the diced onion in the butter until soft.
2. Add the diced red peppers, paprika, salt, and bay leaves to the onion. Simmer the ingredients for a few minutes until heated thoroughly.
3. Add the heavy cream to the pepper mixture and simmer until hot.
4. Remove the bay leaves and blend the sauce with an immersion blender until smooth. Serve immediately.

Cheese Sauce

NUTRITION FACTS   **Makes 6 Servings**

Recipe Yields: 2 cups

Serving Size: ⅓ cup

Each Serving Provides:

2.75:1 Ratio

Calories: 364

Carbohydrate: 2.41 grams

Protein: 10.26 grams

Fat: 34.79 grams

This is a very thick, rich, and creamy cheese sauce. Is some persuasion needed to eat vegetables? This should do the trick! Light olive oil is used in this recipe because it has a neutral flavor. Any other neutral flavor oil will work as well.

240 grams or 1 cup 36% heavy cream

28 grams or 2 tablespoons butter

27 grams or ⅛ cup light olive oil

226 grams or 8 ounces extra sharp cheddar cheese, shredded (about 2¼ cups shredded)

1. Combine the cream, butter, and oil in a heavy-bottomed pot. Heat the cream mixture over low-medium heat until it is hot. Once the cream is hot, whisk in the shredded cheese. Continue to whisk until the cheese is completely melted and the sauce is thoroughly combined. Serve immediately.

Chimichurri Sauce

NUTRITION FACTS **Makes 8 Servings**

Recipe Yields: 1 cup

Serving Size: 2 tablespoons

Each Serving Provides:

20.12:1 Ratio

Calories: 125

Carbohydrate: 0.47 grams

Protein: 0.21 grams

Fat: 13.55 grams

Chimichurri sauce is a full-flavored, herb-infused oil. It is packed with fresh flavors and brightens any dish it is served with.

30 grams or ½ cup chopped parsley

30 grams or ½ cup chopped cilantro, stems and leaves

108 grams or ½ cup extra virgin olive oil

30 grams or 2 tablespoons freshly squeezed lime juice

3.5 grams or ¾ teaspoon Truvia (1 packet)

Pinch of salt

Pinch of garlic powder

1. Combine all of the ingredients in a blender or food processor. Blend until combined, but not completely pureed. Scrape the sides once and blend again. Pour sauce into an airtight jar and serve. Store in the refrigerator.

Guacamole

NUTRITION FACTS **Makes 8 Servings**

Recipe Yields: 1 cup

Serving Size: 2 tablespoons

Each Serving Provides:

2.75:1 Ratio

Calories: 41

Carbohydrate: 0.97 grams

Protein: 0.65 grams

Fat: 4.45 grams

Used as a dip, sauce, or spread, guacamole is an easy way to add a healthy fat to any meal.

230 grams or 1 cup very well mashed Hass avocado (about 2 large avocados)

14 grams or 1 tablespoon minced jalapeño pepper (about 1 medium pepper)

30 grams or 2 tablespoons freshly squeezed lime juice

15 grams or ⅛ cup chopped cilantro, stems and leaves

1.5 grams or ½ teaspoon minced garlic

Salt and pepper to taste

1. Combine the avocado with all remaining ingredients and stir very well to combine.
2. To store the guacamole, place it into a glass bowl, press it down to remove air bubbles, then flatten the top with a fork. Press plastic wrap directly onto of the entire surface of the guacamole and cover with a lid.

Tzatziki Sauce

NUTRITION FACTS **Makes 12 Servings**

Recipe Yields: 1½ cups

Serving Size: 2 tablespoons

Each Serving Provides:

3.15:1 Ratio

Calories: 68

Carbohydrate: 0.89 grams

Protein: 1.20 grams

Fat: 6.60 grams

Fresh and bright are the two words that will come to mind when you taste this sauce. A traditional Mediterranean yogurt-based condiment, tzatziki is often served alongside grilled meats.

115 grams or ½ cup full-fat sour cream

115 grams or ½ cup Fage 2% Plain Greek Yogurt

54 grams or ¼ cup extra virgin olive oil

40 grams or ¼ cup very finely minced cucumber, no seeds

30 grams or 2 tablespoons freshly squeezed lemon juice

5 grams or 1 tablespoon snipped fresh dill sprigs (try fresh spearmint as an alternative)

1. In a bowl, stir all ingredients together very well to combine.

Tahini Dressing

NUTRITION FACTS **Makes 8 Servings**

Recipe Yields: 1 cup

Serving Size: 2 tablespoons

Each Serving Provides:

3.67:1 Ratio

Calories: 231

Carbohydrate: 2.36 grams

Protein: 3.86 grams

Fat: 22.83 grams

A creamy dressing without any dairy. This is especially good served with meat or drizzled on salads.

108 grams or ½ cup canola oil

120 grams or ½ cup tahini paste (100% ground sesame seeds)

18 grams or 1 tablespoon soy sauce

15 grams or 1 tablespoon freshly squeezed lemon juice

0.5 grams or ⅛ teaspoon garlic powder

Optional: liquid stevia drops

1. Combine all ingredients in a Mason jar. Cover tightly with a lid and shake to combine. Store in the refrigerator.

Raspberry Chia Vinaigrette

NUTRITION FACTS **Makes 6 Servings**

Recipe Yields: ¾ cup

Serving Size: 2 tablespoons

Each Serving Provides:

27.84:1 Ratio

Calories: 168

Carbohydrate: 0.39 grams

Protein: 0.27 grams

Fat: 18.42 grams

Use fresh raspberries for the best flavor, but frozen raspberries may be substituted. Light olive oil is specified because it has a mild flavor that does not compete with the raspberries.

108 grams or ½ cup light olive oil

31 grams or ¼ cup raspberries, chopped

30 grams or 2 tablespoons red wine vinegar

7.5 grams or ½ tablespoon whole chia seeds

Tiny pinch of salt

Liquid stevia drops to taste if desired

1. Combine all ingredients together in a Mason jar. Cover with a tight-fitting lid, and shake vigorously to combine. The raspberries will continue to break apart into very small pieces.

2. Let the vinaigrette sit for two hours before serving. This will allow the chia seeds to soften and plump up and the dressing to continue to thicken.

3. Shake very well before serving. Store in a covered glass jar in the refrigerator.

Dijon Vinaigrette

NUTRITION FACTS (with lemon juice) Makes 6 Servings

Recipe Yields: ¾ cup

Serving Size: 2 tablespoons

Each Serving Provides:

19.63:1 Ratio

Calories: 167

Carbohydrate: 0.77 grams

Protein: 0.15 grams

Fat: 18.13 grams

NUTRITION FACTS (with balsamic vinegar) Makes 6 Servings

Recipe yields: ¾ cup

Serving Size: 2 tablespoons

Each Serving Provides:

9.06:1 Ratio

171 calories

Carbohydrate: 1.83 grams

Protein: 0.17 grams

Fat: 18.10 grams

This classic dressing goes with everything! Lemony and bright, it's fantastic on fish and spring vegetables. Try replacing the lemon juice with balsamic vinegar. The balsamic vinegar pairs well with darker greens and meat.

108 grams or ½ cup extra virgin olive oil

61 grams or ¼ cup freshly squeezed lemon juice

15 grams or 1 tablespoon Dijon mustard

3 grams or ½ tablespoon sliced scallions

3.5 grams or ¾ teaspoon Truvia (1 packet)

Salt and pepper to taste

1. In a Mason jar, combine all ingredients. Shake very well to combine, making sure the mustard has completely dissolved. Season to taste. Use immediately or store in the refrigerator tightly sealed.

Bacon Vinaigrette

NUTRITION FACTS **Makes 8 Servings**

Recipe Yields: 1 cup

Serving Size: 2 tablespoons

Each Serving Provides:

4.95:1 Ratio

Calories: 171

Carbohydrate: 0.57 grams

Protein: 2.95 grams

Fat: 17.42 grams

Salad dressing does not get any better than this! For a "secret ingredient" twist, add 1 teaspoon of white truffle–infused oil. The flavor of the truffle oil complements the smokiness of the bacon and makes the dressing a standout.

108 grams or ½ cup extra virgin olive oil

60 grams or ¼ cup cider vinegar (try white balsamic vinegar as an alternative)

56 grams or 2 strips crisp, cooked bacon, crumbled into pieces

15 grams or 1 tablespoon Dijon mustard

15 grams or 1 tablespoon mayonnaise

2 grams or ½ teaspoon Truvia

0.5 grams or ⅛ teaspoon garlic powder

Salt and pepper to taste

Optional: 5 grams or 1 teaspoon white truffle infused olive oil

1. In a small blender cup or a glass container large enough for an immersion blender, combine all of the ingredients. Blend for 15 to 30 seconds or until the dressing has emulsified and the bacon has been chopped into very fine pieces. There should still be small visible pieces of bacon evenly distributed in the dressing.

2. Season the dressing to taste and serve. This is best served at room temperature.

Veggie Ranch Dressing

NUTRITION FACTS Makes 16 Servings

Recipe Yields: 2 cups

Serving Size: 2 tablespoons

Each Serving Provides:

13.55:1 Ratio

Calories: 136

Carbohydrate: 0.71 grams

Protein: 0.37 grams

Fat: 14.61 grams

Pour over a salad or use as a dipping sauce for meat. This recipe is kid and adult friendly.

15 grams or ⅛ cup diced carrots

15 grams or ⅛ cup diced red bell peppers

15 grams or ¼ cup chopped parsley

5 grams or 1 tablespoon sliced scallions

5 grams or ¼ cup snipped dill

15 grams or 1 tablespoon cider vinegar

0.5 grams or ⅛ teaspoon garlic powder

230 grams or 1 cup full-fat sour cream

235 grams or 1 cup mayonnaise

1 teaspoon salt

Optional: 5–10 liquid stevia drops to taste if desired

1. In a food processor, combine the carrots, bell peppers, parsley, scallions, and dill. Chop the vegetables until they are very finely minced. Remove the lid, scrape the sides of the processor, and chop once more.

2. Add the remaining ingredients and blend until completely combined. Scrape the sides once and blend again.

3. Pour into a glass container with a lid and store in the refrigerator.

Thousand Island Dressing

NUTRITION FACTS Makes 12 Servings

Recipe Yields: 1½ cups

Serving Size: 2 tablespoons

Each Serving Provides:

25.99:1 Ratio

Calories: 144

Carbohydrate: 0.49 grams

Protein: 0.12 grams

Fat: 15.68 grams

Thousand Island dressing is really just a combination of three different condiments, mayonnaise, ketchup, and relish. Here, the recipe has been reworked for ketogenic diets by using sugar-free ingredients that still impart the same flavors.

5 grams or ½ tablespoon minced yellow onion

80 grams or ½ cup diced dill pickles

15 grams or 1 tablespoon tomato paste

15 grams or 1 tablespoon cider vinegar

235 grams or 1 cup mayonnaise

0.5 grams or ⅛ teaspoon garlic powder

Optional: liquid stevia drops to taste

1. Using a food processer, finely mince the onion and pickles.
2. Add the remaining ingredients to the food processor and run until completely combined. Scrape the sides once and run again for a few seconds.
3. Refrigerate the dressing in a covered glass jar.

Chili Powder BBQ Sauce

NUTRITION FACTS **Makes 4 Servings**

Recipe Yields: ¼ cup

Serving Size: 1 tablespoon

Each Serving Provides:

0.06:1 Ratio

Calories: 16

Carbohydrate: 2.48 grams

Protein: 0.95 grams

Fat: 0.22 grams

This recipe produces a very thick, concentrated paste enough for 1 pound of meat. Rub onto your choice of meat and grill so the natural sugars in the tomato paste caramelize, creating a flavorful meal. Add a tablespoon of water to make a looser BBQ sauce if desired. Make a large batch and freeze leftover portions in the freezer in ice cube trays.

30 grams or 2 tablespoons tomato paste

18 grams or 1 tablespoon soy sauce

15 grams or 1 tablespoon balsamic vinegar

4 grams or 2 teaspoons chili powder

1 grams or ½ teaspoon paprika

0.5 grams or ⅛ teaspoon garlic powder

0.5 grams or ⅛ teaspoon onion powder

0.5 grams or ⅛ teaspoon cinnamon

0.1 grams or a pinch of ground cloves

¼ teaspoon salt

Optional: 5 drops liquid stevia

1. In a small bowl, whisk together the tomato paste, soy sauce, and balsamic vinegar.
2. Add the dry spices and liquid stevia drops, if desired, to the tomato mixture and stir to combine. Use immediately or freeze in individual portions.

Low-Carbohydrate Salsa

NUTRITION FACTS **Makes 8 Servings**

Recipe Yields: 1 cup

Serving Size: 2 tablespoons

Each Serving Provides:

0.11:1 Ratio

Calories: 15

Carbohydrate: 2.61 grams

Protein: 0.44 grams

Fat: 0.35 grams

You will not miss the bland salsa that comes in a jar! This recipe is fresh and bright. It is so easy and quick to make, you will wonder why you never tried before.

250 grams or 1 cup canned tomato

56 grams or ¼ cup canned chili peppers

40 grams or ¼ cup diced onion

30 grams or 2 tablespoons freshly squeezed lime juice

15 grams or ¼ cup chopped cilantro, stems and leaves

salt and pepper to taste

Optional: red pepper flakes

1. Place all of the ingredients in a blender or food processor. Blend until completely combined. The onions and cilantro should be evenly chopped and distributed throughout the salsa. Season with salt, pepper, and red pepper flakes, if desired. Pour into a Mason jar, cover, and refrigerate.

Tomatillo Salsa

NUTRITION FACTS   **Makes 16 Servings**

Recipe Yields: 2 cups

Serving Size: 2 tablespoons

Each Serving Provides:

0.17:1 Ratio

Calories: 12

Carbohydrate: 1.72 grams

Protein: 0.42 grams

Fat: 0.37 grams

Tomatillos look like green tomatoes covered with a paper husk. If they feel sticky under the husk, wash them under cold water.

454 grams or 1 pound fresh tomatillos

113 grams or 1 (4-ounce) can diced chilies

40 grams or ¼ cup diced onion

3 grams or 1 teaspoon minced garlic

30 grams or ½ cup chopped cilantro, stems and leaves

Pinch of salt

1. Remove the paper husks and wash the tomatillos. Cut them in halves and quarters so all the pieces are about the same size.

2. In a pot, combine the tomatillos, chilies, onion, and garlic. Add enough water to the pot so the tomatillos are just barely covered. The tomatillos float, so be careful not to add too much water!

3. Bring the tomatillo mixture to a boil. Reduce the heat to keep the mixture at a high simmer. Simmer for about 30 minutes or until the tomatillos are completely cooked through and easily mashed with a fork.

4. Add the cilantro and salt to the cooked tomatillo mixture and use an immersion blender to puree the salsa into a chunky consistency. Pour the cooked salsa into a glass container and cover tightly. Allow to cool before serving or freezing.

Kale Pesto

NUTRITION FACTS   **Makes 24 Servings**

Recipe Yields: 1½ cups

Serving Size: 1 tablespoon

Each Serving Provides:

4.71:1 Ratio

Calories: 63

Carbohydrate: 0.54 grams

Protein: 0.82 grams

Fat: 6.42 grams

Pesto with a powder boost from nutrient dense kale! Always have a batch of this on hand to add flavor to meat, vegetables, and even eggs. Freeze small portions in ice cube trays for longer storage.

45 grams or 2 cups packed chopped curly kale

60 grams or ½ cup English walnut pieces

3 grams or 1 teaspoon minced garlic

25 grams or ¼ cup grated Parmesan cheese

61 grams or ¼ cup freshly squeezed lemon juice

108 grams or ½ cup extra virgin olive oil

Salt and pepper to taste

Optional: Truvia to taste (to help counter some of the kale's bitterness)

1. Combine the chopped kale, walnuts, garlic, and Parmesan cheese in a food processor. Pulse five to six times to coarsely chop the kale and walnuts.

2. Add the lemon juice and run the processor on high. Pour the olive oil through the lid spout in a steady, slow stream until all of the oil is incorporated. The kale should be very finely minced and all ingredients emulsified.

3. Taste the pesto for seasoning and add salt, pepper, and Truvia, if desired.

4. Pour into an airtight jar and store in the refrigerator.

Classic Tartar Sauce

NUTRITION FACTS **Makes 8 Servings**

Recipe Yields: 1 cup

Serving Size: 2 tablespoons

Each Serving Provides:

54:1 Ratio

Calories: 160

Carbohydrate: 0.27 grams

Protein: 0.06 grams

Fat: 17.61 grams

Use dill pickles minced finely in place of sugar-filled relish. If you like your sauce slightly sweeter, use a few drops of liquid stevia.

176 grams or ¾ cup mayonnaise

60 grams or ¼ cup finely minced dill pickles

Pepper to taste

Optional: a few drops of liquid stevia

1. Combine all of the ingredients in a small bowl. Cover tightly and store in the refrigerator.

Miso Butter

Recipe Yields: ½ cup

Serving Size: 1 tablespoon

Each Serving Provides:

11.14:1 Ratio

Calories: 107

Carbohydrate: 0.61 grams

Protein: 0.42 grams

Fat: 11.46 grams

Miso butter adds a unique flavor to vegetables and proteins. It goes especially well with Asian seasonings.

113 grams or 1 stick of butter, room temperature

24 grams or 4 teaspoons white miso paste

1. In a small bowl, stir the butter and miso paste together until well combined. Store the butter in a covered glass dish and keep refrigerated.

Peanut Sauce

NUTRITION FACTS **Makes 4 Servings**

Recipe Yields: ½ cup

Serving Size: ⅛ cup

Each Serving Provides:

2.85:1 Ratio

Calories: 132

Carbohydrate: 2.26 grams

Protein: 2.19 grams

Fat: 12.66 grams

Use crunchy peanut butter if you would like a little texture in your sauce. Add red pepper flakes for a spicier version.

30 grams or 2 tablespoons coconut milk, full-fat and unsweetened

30 grams or 2 tablespoons canola oil

30 grams or 2 tablespoons peanut butter, unsweetened, peanuts only

15 grams or 1 tablespoon soy sauce

15 grams or 1 tablespoon cider vinegar

5 grams or 1 teaspoon very finely minced fresh ginger root

0.5 grams or ⅛ teaspoon garlic powder

1. In a small bowl, whisk together all of the ingredients until well combined. Store in the refrigerator in a covered jar.

TREATS AND DESSERTS

Dark Chocolate Candies

Caramel Sauce

Refrigerator Coconut Macaroons

Coconut–Lime Popsicles

Cucumber–Mint Popsicles

Cinnamon Chayote Squash

Frozen Orange Cream Delights

Vanilla Pudding

Chocolate Chia Pudding

Fluffy and Light Vanilla Cupcakes

Coffee Cake

Peanut Butter Cookies

Marshmallows

Dark Chocolate Candies

NUTRITION FACTS **Makes 12 Servings**

Recipe Yields: 12 candies

Serving Size: 1 candy

Each Serving Provides:

4.66:1 Ratio

Calories: 56

Carbohydrate: 0.83 grams

Protein: 0.38 grams

Fat: 5.65 grams

Chocolate makes people happy! It can be even more fun when you make it yourself. Silicone chocolate molds are inexpensive and make for an impressive presentation. Homemade chocolates are easy to fill with a variety of raw ingredients including macadamia nuts, pistachios, chopped almonds, unsweetened coconut, or even chia seeds. You can also easily fill the chocolates with prepared caramel sauce, chocolate chia pudding, coconut macaroon, or nut butters. The combinations are limitless!

Truvia and liquid stevia were both tested. Liquid stevia had a very bitter aftertaste when combined with the chocolate. Truvia results in better flavor, but it can be challenging to dissolve in the heavy cream because it is high in fat. The key is to heat the heavy cream until it is very hot. Continue to stir until all the granules of Truvia have dissolved.

55 grams or ¼ cup melted cacao butter

30 grams or 2 tablespoons 36% heavy cream

10 grams or 2 teaspoons Truvia (add more if you like the chocolate sweeter)

5 grams or 1 teaspoon pure vanilla extract

Pinch of salt

20 grams or ¼ cup Hershey's unsweetened cocoa powder

1. In a small pot over very low heat, melt the cacao butter.
2. In a small bowl, combine the heavy cream, Truvia, vanilla extract, and salt. Stir well to combine. Microwave the cream mixture in 5-second intervals until the cream is very hot. Stir after each heating. Continue to stir until all the Truvia granules have dissolved.
3. In a glass measuring cup with a spout, combine the melted cacao butter, heavy cream mixture, and cocoa powder. Stir until it is very smooth and shiny with no lumps remaining.
4. Pour the chocolate into the molds and allow it to harden. Do not refrigerate to speed up the process. Let the chocolates sit for one day before eating them. This will help the chocolate flavors to mellow and combine.

To add fillings inside of the chocolate candies, fill the molds half way. Allow the chocolate to begin to set up for a few minutes. Next, add nuts or fillings by placing a very small amount in the center of each chocolate. Gently push it into the chocolate so it is lower than the top of the mold. A toothpick or wet fingers (for sticky fillings) are helpful for this part. The chocolate should push up the sides of the mold, encasing the filling. Add additional chocolate if necessary to reach the top of the mold and cover the filling.

Caramel Sauce

NUTRITION FACTS   **Makes 8 Servings**

Recipe Yields: 1 cup

Serving Size: ⅛ cup

Each Serving Provides:

19.04:1 Ratio

Calories: 162

Carbohydrate: 0.51 grams

Protein: 0.41 grams

Fat: 17.61 grams

You will be amazed! These three common ingredients combined in a unique way produce a caramel sauce that will leave you wanting more. This is the most popular recipe I have ever created—check out a video tutorial of me making this recipe on www.charliefoundation.org. Use salted butter for a "salted caramel" flavor or unsalted butter for a traditional caramel flavor. This recipe is easy to reduce or double, just use equal parts heavy cream to butter.

The sauce will remain pourable at room temperature. If a pourable consistency is desired, it is best enjoyed right away. When refrigerated, the sauce will harden to the consistency of butter. This is ideal for making small candies. It is not possible to reheat the sauce once it has hardened. Unfortunately, the sauce will separate.

114 grams or 1 stick butter

120 grams or ½ cup 40% heavy cream

20 grams or 1 tablespoon plus 1 teaspoon Truvia

Optional: pinch of salt

1. Melt the butter in a small nonstick pan over medium low heat. Use a whisk and continuously stir until it is a light brown color.

2. Add the cream, Truvia, and salt if using, to the butter. The cream will bubble and foam when added to the butter—this is OK! Continue to whisk until it begins to feel sticky and the sauce has thickened, about one to two minutes.

3. Remove the pan from the heat and continue to stir until it has cooled slightly.

4. Allow it to cool a little more before serving. If refrigerated, the sauce will harden.

Refrigerator Coconut Macaroons

NUTRITION FACTS **Makes 24 Servings**

Recipe Yields: 24 macaroons

Serving Size: 1 macaroon

Each Serving Provides:

4.54:1 Ratio

Calories: 35

Carbohydrate: 0.44 grams

Protein: 0.34 grams

Fat: 3.54 grams

Looking for a no fuss, no bake dessert that satisfies the sweet tooth? Refrigerator Coconut Macaroons are the perfect option!

113 grams or ½ cup coconut milk, full-fat and unsweetened

100 grams or 1 cup finely shredded dried coconut, unsweetened

7 grams or 1½ teaspoons Truvia (2 packets)

1. In a mixing bowl, stir together all ingredients until very well combined and there are no lumps of dried coconut. Pack the mixture down as much as possible. Cover with plastic wrap and let the mixture rest for two hours or overnight.

2. Use a melon baller or other small round scoop to dish out small rounds. Arrange the rounds in one even layer in a large plastic container. Separate each layer with a piece of waxed or parchment paper. Cover and refrigerate.

Coconut–Lime Popsicles

NUTRITION FACTS **Makes 6 Servings**

Serving Size: ⅓ cup

Each Serving Provides:

2.72:1 Ratio

Calories: 67

Carbohydrate: 1.69 grams

Protein: 0.64 grams

Fat: 6.35 grams

Some individuals may be resistant to eating avocado. This is the perfect recipe to sneak this super food in. The lime juice and sweetener transform the avocado into a refreshing dessert. The green color won't even be questioned!

115 grams or ½ cup mashed avocado

113 grams or ½ cup coconut milk, full-fat and unsweetened

61 grams or ¼ cup freshly squeezed lime juice

7 grams or 1½ teaspoons Truvia (2 packets)

Up to ¾ cup additional water

1. Combine all ingredients in a blender. Blend until completely smooth. Make sure you have 2 cups of liquid total. If not, you may add more water to reach 2 cups.
2. Pour ⅓ cup of the mixture into six popsicle molds. Freeze overnight or until completely solid.

Cucumber–Mint Popsicles

NUTRITION FACTS   **Makes 6 Servings**

Recipe Yields: 3 cups

Serving Size: ½ cup

Each Serving Provides:

1.5:1 Ratio

Calories: 40

Carbohydrate: 1.80 grams

Protein: 0.50 grams

Fat: 3.44 grams

Feel like a cool refreshing treat but don't want something overly sweet? Cucumber–Mint Popsicles are a great choice! Enjoy one of these cool and refreshing popsicles on a hot summer day.

240 grams or 2 cups finely diced English cucumber with peel

1 cup water

113 grams or ½ cup coconut milk, full-fat and unsweetened

2 grams or 16 fresh mint leaves

7 grams or 1½ teaspoons Truvia (2 packets)

1. Combine all ingredients in a blender and blend on full speed until completely pureed.

2. Pour ½ cup of the mixture into each of six popsicle molds and freeze overnight.

Cinnamon Chayote Squash

NUTRITION FACTS **Makes 4 Servings**

Recipe Yields: 2 cups

Serving Size: ½ cup

Each Serving Provides:

2.68:1 Ratio

Calories: 120

Carbohydrate: 3.50 grams

Protein: 0.78 grams

Fat: 11.47 grams

Vegetables for dessert! If you have never tried this type of squash before, don't be afraid. It has a very neutral flavor and the texture when cooked is similar to cooked green apples. It's a great way to "hit the sweet spot" and enjoy the flavors of an apple pie without the high carbs. Chayote squash has a natural thickening quality similar to okra when it is cooked. If the mixture becomes too thick, add a little more water.

300 grams or 2 cups peeled and sliced thin chayote squash

56 grams or ½ stick butter

4 grams or ½ tablespoon ground cinnamon (or try a pie spice blend)

10 grams or 2 teaspoons Truvia

Pinch of salt

2 cups water

Optional: dash of pure vanilla extract

1. In a pot over medium heat, combine all of the ingredients and bring to a full simmer. Simmer for 30 minutes or until the water has reduced by half and the sauce has thickened. The squash should be very tender.

2. Allow the mixture to cool before serving. Top with whipped heavy cream for additional fat.

Frozen Orange Cream Delights

NUTRITION FACTS   **Makes 6 Servings**

Recipe Yields: 2 cups

Serving Size: ⅓ cup

Each Serving Provides:

1.52:1 Ratio

Calories: 60

Carbohydrate: 2.91 grams

Protein: 0.48 grams

Fat: 5.14 grams

So simple and so delicious! A great treat to have on hand during the summer.

170 grams or ¾ cup coconut milk, full-fat and unsweetened

124 grams or ½ cup freshly squeezed orange juice

7 grams or 1½ teaspoons Truvia (2 packets)

¾ cup water

1. Combine all ingredients in a 2-cup glass measuring cup. It is helpful if the measuring cup has a spout. Stir very well until completely combined and the Truvia has dissolved.
2. Pour ⅓ cup of the mixture into each of six popsicle molds and freeze overnight.

Vanilla Pudding

NUTRITION FACTS   **Makes 8 Servings**

Recipe Yields: 2 cups

Serving Size: ¼ cup

Each Serving Provides:

4.36:1 Ratio

Calories: 235

Carbohydrate: 2.89 grams

Protein: 2.54 grams

Fat: 23.68 grams

Just like you always remembered, but better! In place of milk, this recipe uses an entire 2 cups of heavy cream, so it is extra rich and delicious. Best of all, it is ready in 30 minutes. This is best served warm. The arrowroot flour will have a rough or sandy texture after it has cooled. Gently warm the pudding in a double boiler if it has been refrigerated.

476 grams or 2 cups 36% heavy cream

68 grams or 4 large egg yolks

14 grams or 3 teaspoons Truvia (4 packets)

6 grams or 2 teaspoons arrowroot flour

5 grams or 1 teaspoon pure vanilla extract

Pinch of salt

1. In a heavy-bottomed pot, whisk together all of the ingredients, making sure the egg yolks are completely combined. I recommend using a small whisk that can reach into the corners of the pot.

2. Place the pot over medium heat and stir constantly with a whisk making sure to scrape the bottom and sides of the pot. Once the pudding mixture begins to steam, reduce the heat to low.

3. Continue to cook the pudding for about 10 minutes, continuously stirring and scraping the bottom and sides. After about 10 minutes, it should be thick enough to leave a trail with the back of a spoon.

4. Pour the pudding through a mesh sieve into eight ramekins or small cups. Let it cool for about 15 minutes and serve warm. To store, press plastic wrap onto the surface of the pudding to prevent a "skin" from forming. Cover tightly and store in the refrigerator.

Chocolate Chia Pudding

NUTRITION FACTS **Makes 6 Servings**

Recipe Yield: 1½ cups

Serving Size: ¼ cup

Each Serving Provides:

2.73:1 Ratio

Calories: 86

Carbohydrate: 1.67 grams

Protein: 1.33 grams

Fat: 8.20 grams

When added to liquid, chia seeds swell and create a thick gel. They are the perfect ingredient for a no-cook chocolate pudding.

226 grams or 1 cup coconut milk, full-fat and unsweetened

26 grams or 2 tablespoons whole chia seeds

5 grams or 1 tablespoon Hershey's Cocoa Powder, unsweetened

7 grams or 1½ teaspoons Truvia (2 packets)

½ cup water

1. In a bowl, whisk together all of the ingredients making sure there are no lumps of cocoa powder or coconut milk. Cover the bowl and refrigerate overnight to allow the chia seeds to soften.

2. After sitting overnight, give the pudding another good stir. Divide it into six portions, cover, and store in the refrigerator.

Fluffy and Light Vanilla Cupcakes

NUTRITION FACTS **Makes 12 Servings**

Recipe Yields: 12 cupcakes

Serving Size: 1 cupcake

Each Serving Provides:

1.25:1 Ratio

Calories: 119 calories

Carbohydrate: 3.82 grams

Protein: 3.95 grams

Fat: 9.72 grams

Every once in a while, you just need a little cake! Make an entire batch for a party or make just one. You will not be disappointed with this recipe. The key is to work fast, prep your tools, have the oven ready, and premeasure your ingredients. The dry ingredients will absorb the oil very fast and you'll want to incorporate the egg whites before the batter becomes too stiff. So please read all the steps of this recipe before diving in! Don't want to make a large batch? Half of the recipe provides enough batter for six cupcakes or one 9-inch cake. See the box on the following page for a single serving ingredient list.

360 grams or 12 large egg whites (discard yolks)

108 grams or ½ cup canola oil (do not use coconut oil, it will solidify too quickly)

5 grams or 1 teaspoon pure vanilla extract

56 grams or ½ cup coconut flour

32 grams or ¼ cup arrowroot flour

49 grams or a ¼ cup Truvia (14 packets)

5 grams or 1 teaspoon baking powder

5 grams or 1 teaspoon baking soda

0.5 grams or ⅛ teaspoon xanthan gum

Pinch of salt

1. Preheat the oven to 300°F. Prepare a muffin pan by placing one parchment paper liner in each well.

2. Place all 12 egg whites into a large mixing bowl. Use an electric hand mixer to whip the eggs into stiff peaks. Set aside.

3. Combine the canola oil and vanilla extract in a second mixing bowl. To the wet ingredients, sift in the coconut flour, arrowroot flour, Truvia, baking powder, baking soda, xanthan gum, and salt. Use a silicone spatula to quickly combine the wet and dry ingredients. The dry ingredients will absorb the moisture

almost immediately. Use the side of the spatula to make sure there are no lumps or dry ingredients in the batter.

4. Scoop about a quarter of the whipped egg whites into the coconut flour mixture. Stir very well to combine; the batter will continue to thicken rapidly, keep stirring!

5. Add another quarter of the egg whites to the coconut flour mixture and begin to fold the ingredients together. Use a silicone spatula to divide the batter in half, scrape the bottom of the bowl and fold the bottom of the batter over the top until the egg whites are incorporated—about five to six times.

6. Repeat the same folding process two more times with the remaining egg whites, adding a quarter of the egg whites each time. Use a whisk if absolutely necessary to break up any remaining batter lumps. It is OK if there are small spots of egg white.

7. Once all of the egg whites are incorporated, use a spoon or a portion scoop to fill the cupcake liners about three quarters of the way full. You should have 12 equal cupcakes. Bake for 30 minutes. Do not be tempted to open the oven door or rotate the pan! This will cause the cupcakes not to rise as high.

8. After baking, let the cupcakes cool in the pan for about 15 minutes and then carefully remove them to a cooling rack. Once cool, store these in an airtight container.

For One Fluffy and Light Vanilla Cupcake
30 grams or 1 large egg white (discard yolk)
10 grams or 2 teaspoons canola oil
1 gram or 5 drops pure vanilla extract
5 grams or ½ tablespoon coconut flour
3 grams or 1 teaspoon arrowroot flour
3.5 grams or ¾ teaspoon Truvia (1 packet)
0.5 grams or ⅛ teaspoon baking powder
0.5 grams or ⅛ teaspoon baking soda
A tiny pinch of xanthan gum
A tiny pinch of salt
Follow the same process as for the full recipe, using smaller mixing bowls.

Coffee Cake

NUTRITION FACTS **Makes 12 Servings**

Recipe Yields: Two 9-inch cakes

Serving Size: ⅙ of one cake

Each Serving Provides

1.95:1 Ratio

Calories: 273

Carbohydrate: 5.21 grams

Protein: 7.48 grams

Fat: 24.73 grams

Enjoy this classic dessert without all of the carbs! This cake uses the same recipe as Fluffy and Light Vanilla Cupcakes (page 132) except the egg yolks are reserved and transformed into a cinnamon streusel topping. The listed serving sizes are very generous. If the carb allotment is too high, half of a serving will still be enough for a treat!

1 batch of Fluffy and Light Vanilla Cupcake batter (page 132)

204 grams or 12 egg yolks

113 grams or 1 stick butter, room temperature

28 grams or ¼ cup almond meal

28 grams or ¼ cup crushed pecans

14 grams or 2 tablespoons cinnamon (reserve a little for sprinkling on top if desired)

14 grams or 3 teaspoons Truvia (4 packets)

5 grams or 1 teaspoon pure vanilla extract

1. Preheat the oven to 350°F. Grease the bottom and sides of two 9-inch pans with butter. Cut parchment paper to fit the bottom of the pans and line the buttered pans.

2. In a mixing bowl, combine the egg yolks, butter, almond meal, pecans, cinnamon, Truvia, and vanilla extract with an electric hand mixer. It is OK if there is egg white mixture on the beaters from making the Fluffy and Light Vanilla Cupcake batter.

3. Pour the prepared vanilla cupcake batter into the two lined pans. Drop evenly spaced spoonful's of the cinnamon mixture on top of the vanilla cake batter. Use half of the cinnamon mixture for each cake pan.

Use a knife to swirl the cinnamon mixture into the cake batter. Do not completely mix the cinnamon mixture into the cake batter; you want to create a "swirled" effect.

4. Bake the cake for 30 minutes or until a toothpick inserted into the center comes out clean. Allow the cakes to cool for 15 to 20 minutes before cutting each cake into six slices.

Peanut Butter Cookies

NUTRITION FACTS **Makes 16 Servings**

Recipe Yields: 16 cookies

Serving Size: 1 cookie

Each Serving Provides

2.99:1 Ratio

Calories: 104

Carbohydrate: 1.13 grams

Protein: 2.25 grams

Fat: 10.09 grams

A childhood favorite! Peanut Butter Cookies are among the easiest desserts to make. With just a handful of ingredients and a few minutes of time you will have a dessert to satisfy a sweet craving. For an extra rich dessert, spread 1 to 2 teaspoons of Caramel Sauce (page 124) between two cookies to create a caramel peanut butter cookie sandwich. Use chunky or smooth peanut butter depending on what you like!

129 grams or ½ cup peanut butter, unsweetened, peanuts only

113 grams or 1 stick butter, room temperature

50 grams or 1 large egg

14 grams or 3 teaspoons Truvia (4 packets)

4 grams or 2 teaspoons coconut flour

1. Preheat the oven to 350°F. Line a baking sheet with parchment paper.
2. In a glass mixing bowl, combine all ingredients using an electric hand mixer. Scrape the sides and mix again.
3. Use a tablespoon to scoop 16 scoops of cookie dough onto the baking sheet. Space the cookies about 2 inches apart. Bake for 10 to 12 minutes. The edges should be golden brown and crispy.
4. Allow the cookies to cool for about five minutes on the baking sheet. Use a thin spatula to transfer them to a cooling rack. Once completely cool, store in an airtight plastic container.

Marshmallows

Recipe Yields: 16 marshmallows

Serving Size: 1 marshmallow

Each Serving Provides

1.46:1 Ratio

Calories: 63

Carbohydrate: 1.00 grams

Protein: 2.67 grams

Fat: 5.37 grams

Marshmallows are so easy to make, and you will be glad you did! These are light, fluffy, and closely resemble the sugary ones from the store. The most delicious way to add fat to marshmallows is to dip them in the melted chocolate from the Dark Chocolate Candies recipe (page 122). This is the best low-carb marshmallow recipe you will ever try!

Please use pasteurized eggs in the shell to make this recipe since the egg whites will be eaten raw. Pasteurized eggs may take longer to whip into stiff peaks. Use a metal or glass bowl that is completely clean and dry. Any fat on the bowl or mixer will prevent the whites from whipping. Allow the eggs to come to room temperature in the shell before whipping. Use a stand mixer or an electric hand mixer. The process could take up to 10 minutes.

238 grams or 1 cup 36% heavy cream

29 grams or 8 teaspoons (4 packets unflavored gelatin powder)

8 grams or 1 tablespoon arrowroot flour

14 grams or 3 teaspoons Truvia (4 packets)

5 grams or 1 teaspoon pure vanilla extract

Pinch of salt

120 grams or 4 large egg whites

1. Prepare a 9 × 9-inch glass baking dish by lining the bottom with parchment paper. The sides do not have to be lined.

2. Place the egg whites into a large glass or metal mixing bowl and whip on high speed until they have formed stiff peaks. Set the egg whites aside.

3. In a cold pot, whisk together the heavy cream, gelatin, Truvia, arrowroot powder, and salt. Set the pot over medium low heat. Gently heat until the gelatin has dissolved. The mixture will be very thick and sticky.

4. Mix the gelatin mixture into the egg whites by pouring a very slow steady stream of gelatin mixture into the egg whites. While you are pouring the mixture, run the mixer on low speed to incorporate the gelatin into the eggs. Scrape the sides of the bowl once and mix again. The egg mixture should be thick and shiny.

5. Pour the egg mixture into the glass baking dish and refrigerate until firm, about two hours. Using a sharp knife, slice the marshmallow into 16 squares. Separate the marshmallows and store in an airtight container in the refrigerator.

BEVERAGES

Half and Half Iced Tea

Chia Fresca

Electrolyte Replacement Water

Thai Iced Tea

Half and Half Iced Tea

NUTRITION FACTS **Make 16 Servings**

Recipe Yields: 1 gallon

Serving Size: 8 ounces

Decaffeinated tea is considered a "free" beverage.

1 tablespoon of lemon juice has 1 gram of carbohydrate

No, this is not "Southern Sweet Tea," but add a squeeze of lemon and a few ice cubes and you have a refreshing drink for a hot day. Over time, you will adjust to the lack of sweetness and begin to actually taste the tea! Use liquid stevia drops if you need to, but reduce the amount little by little over time as your taste adjusts.

4 bags decaffeinated green tea

4 bags decaffeinated black tea

1 gallon of water, divided in half

1. In a pot with a lid, bring ½ gallon of water to a full boil. Once the water has boiled, turn off the heat and place all eight tea bags into the hot water. Do not submerge the tags. Cover the pot with a lid and let tea sit overnight or until it is room temperature.

2. Remove and discard the tea bags and pour the tea into a 1 gallon pitcher. Add the remaining water and refrigerate until it is cold.

3. Serve with a lemon wedge and ice.

Chia Fresca

NUTRITION FACTS **Makes 8 servings**

Recipe Yields: 2 quarts

Serving Size: 8 ounces

0.75:1 Ratio

Calories: 15 calories

Carbohydrate: 0.79 grams

Protein: 0.56 grams

Fat: 1.02 grams

Bored with plain water? Try Chia Fresca. It tastes like slightly sweet lemon water. The hydrated chia seeds don't add any flavor, but they swell and create a gelatinous outer layer that you can chew. For an extra refreshing twist, use sparkling mineral water, but if you do, be sure to mix gently with a spoon and not shake.

2 quarts water

26 grams or 2 tablespoons whole chia seeds

61 grams or ¼ cup freshly squeezed lemon juice

Optional: 7 grams or 1½ teaspoons Truvia

1. In a 2-quart glass container, combine all ingredients. If using plain water, shake very well or stir with a whisk; if using carbonated water, stir gently with a spoon. Refrigerate and serve cold. Be sure to stir immediately before serving.

Electrolyte Replacement Water

NUTRITION FACTS   **Makes 4 Servings**

Recipe Yields: 1 quart

Serving Size: 8 ounces

Recipe Provides:

700 milligrams Potassium

1,500 milligrams Chlorine

27 milliequivalents Bicarbonate

1,200 milligrams Sodium

Staying hydrated while on a ketogenic diet is very important. You can make a simple electrolyte replacement beverage at home with a few simple ingredients. The nutrients listed above are similar to what is provided in commercial electrolyte replacement beverages. The main ingredients are shelf stable and should always be kept on hand in case of illness. The bonus is, you control the ingredients and are able to eliminate artificial colors, sweeteners, and preservatives. This beverage may also be used on very hot days or when you may be perspiring a lot. This is considered a "free" beverage when electrolyte replacement is necessary.

Add flavor to the beverage by using liquid stevia drops for sweetness or the zest from lemons, limes, or oranges. The zest will infuse the beverage with the "essence" of the citrus without adding extra carbohydrate.

4 cups filtered water

½ teaspoon baking soda

½ teaspoon Morton Lite Salt

Optional: liquid stevia

Optional: citrus zest

1. Dissolve the salts in the water. Add optional flavorings if desired.

2. Drink 8 ounces every two hours when needed.

Thai Iced Tea

NUTRITION FACTS **Makes 1 Serving**

Recipe Yields: 16 ounces

Serving Size: 16 ounces

4.87:1 Ratio

Calories: 99

Carbohydrate: 1.41 grams

Protein: 0.66 grams

Fat: 10.08 grams

Traditional blends of Thai tea contain an artificial orange coloring. Use regular decaffeinated black tea bags or try vanilla-infused herbal tea. The beverage will not have the same color, but it will taste just as good!

12 ounces brewed and cooled decaffeinated tea (stronger is better)

56 grams or ¼ cup coconut milk, full-fat and unsweetened

Ice

Optional: liquid stevia drops (use vanilla flavor drops if you do not have vanilla infused tea)

1. Pour the brewed tea over the ice in a 20-ounce or larger cup.
2. Pour the coconut milk over the tea and stir. Add liquid stevia drops if using. Enjoy!

Acknowledgments

Thank you Jim and Nancy Abrahams for founding The Charlie Foundation and bringing awareness of the ketogenic diet to those who need it the most. Charlotte's life and thousands of others have been saved because of your work promoting the diet as a "first line treatment" for pediatric epilepsy.

Thank you also for your support in sharing my ketogenic recipes on The Charlie Foundation website. Being able to see pictures of the recipes and visualize what the diet consists of has most definitely made ketogenic diet therapies more approachable to those considering them.

This book and our personal success with ketogenic diet therapy have been made possible by keto dietitian extraordinaire, Beth Zupec-Kania, RDN, CD. Beth's 20 plus years of experience with ketogenic diet therapies and work in developing and maintaining the KetoDietCalculator© has been instrumental in the mainstream acceptance of diet therapy. Words cannot summarize the difference you have made in so many lives.

Index

About the Authors

Dawn Marie Martenz is an Air Force wife and a mother of two, currently residing in Washington, DC. Her daughter, Charlotte Martenz, was diagnosed with Dravet's Syndrome in 2007 and was subsequently started on the ketogenic diet in June 2010. Since starting the diet, Dawn worked tirelessly to fine tune its performance for optimal seizure control for Charlotte. In 2011, Dawn collaborated with Laura Cramp, RD, from Children's National Medical Center in Washington, DC to write *The Keto Cookbook*, the first book dedicated entirely to ketogenic recipes at the 4:1 ratio. Dawn innovated new, flavorful, and aesthetically pleasing ketogenic recipes to improve the palatability of the diet while maintaining overall compliance and adherence. Following the success of the book, www.ketocook.com was created as a means to continue sharing recipes with families worldwide. Currently, Dawn has partnered with The Charlie Foundation for Ketogenic Therapies to continue providing high quality, dietitian-approved recipes for all types of ketogenic diet therapies. She regularly attends conferences and offers ketogenic cooking demonstrations. She is dedicated to continued efforts of creating enjoyable and reliable recipes and helping others become successful in their journey of ketogenic diet therapies.

Beth Zupec-Kania is a Registered Dietitian and Nutritionist who works to promote safe and effective use of ketogenic therapies. She has written many publications and designed KetoDietCalculator©, a web-based program for calculating ketogenic diets. Beth is a consultant to *The Charlie Foundation for Ketogenic Therapies* and has provided ketogenic training to over 150 medical centers worldwide. She feels privileged to be involved in the lives of people who have tried ketogenic diet therapies. Their cooperation and diligence has fueled her efforts to educate the community and professionals to make the diet more available, easier to manage, and more delicious. With research underway on the impact of ketogenic diets in many different conditions, it is her greatest hope that these special diets evolve to the level of disease prevention.